Pocket
BALI

TOP EXPERIENCES • LOCAL LIFE • MADE EASY

Ryan Ver Berkmoes

In This Book

QuickStart Guide

Your keys to understanding the region – we help you decide what to do and how to do it

Need to Know
Tips for a smooth trip

Regions
What's where

Explore Bali

The best things to see and do, area by area

Top Experiences
Make the most of your visit

Local Life
The insider's island

The Best of Bali

The island's highlights in handy lists to help you plan

Best Walks
See the region on foot

Bali's Best...
The best experiences

Survival Guide

Tips and tricks for a seamless, hassle-free island experience

Getting Around
Travel like a local

Essential Information
Including where to stay

Our selection of the island's best places to eat, drink and enjoy:

◎ **Experiences**

✖ **Eating**

🔂 **Drinking**

★ **Entertainment**

🔒 **Shopping**

These symbols give you the vital information for each listing:

🗐 Telephone Numbers	👪 Family-Friendly
🕑 Opening Hours	🐾 Pet-Friendly
🅿 Parking	🚌 Bus
🚭 Nonsmoking	⛴ Ferry
@ Internet Access	Ⓜ Metro
📶 Wi-Fi Access	Ⓢ Subway
🥦 Vegetarian Selection	🚊 Tram
📖 English-Language Menu	🚆 Train

Find each listing quickly on maps for each area:

Bar Hemingway
16 ▢ Map p233, B2

Legend has it that Hemi self, wielding a machine erate this timber-pan ered bar during showpiece is a en by Papa ar town. Dress s.com; Hôtel Rit 🕑6.30pm-2a

6 ◎ Plac Vc

Lonely Planet's Bali

Lonely Planet Pocket Guides are designed to get you straight to the heart of the region.

Inside you'll find all the must-see experiences, plus tips to make your visit to each one really memorable. We've split the island into easy-to-navigate areas and provided clear maps so you'll find your way around with ease. Our expert authors have searched out the best of the region: walks, food, nightlife and shopping, to name a few. Because you want to explore, our 'Local Life' pages will take you to some of the most exciting areas to experience the real Bali.

And of course you'll find all the practical tips you need for a smooth trip: itineraries for short visits, how to get around, and how much to tip the guy who serves you a drink at the end of a long day's exploration.

It's your guarantee of a really great experience.

Our Promise

You can trust our travel information because Lonely Planet authors visit the places we write about, each and every edition. We never accept freebies for positive coverage, so you can rely on us to tell it like it is.

QuickStart Guide

Welcome to Bali

Bali is like no other destination in the world. Its rich culture plays out at all levels of life, from the exquisite flower-petal offerings placed everywhere to the processions of joyfully garbed locals to the otherworldly traditional music and dance performed island-wide. Add in beaches, surfing, great dining, killer sunsets, beautiful walks, fabulous shopping, and more, Bali is unbeatable.

Ferries moored at Sanur (p82)
DENNIS WALTON/LONELY PLANET IMAGES ©

⊙ Bali
Top Experiences

Feeling Spiritual at Pura Luhur Batukau (p58)

A multitiered temple like something out of Kyoto rises out of the mists cloaking the side of one of Bali's main volcanoes. You've reached Pura Luhur Batukau, where you can feel the island's sacred magic.

Hanging Out at Ulu Watu's Beaches (p68)

Bali's own version of pearls, the string of beaches towards Ulu Watu has some of the island's best sand shimmering in the sunlight. Enjoy the adventure of reaching these often remote locations.

Gili Trawangan
(p124)

An all-day, all-night party, that's Gili T. Sure, divers can find briny joy and snorkellers can enjoy beauty right off the beach, but really, take a fast boat over to whoop it up.

Nusa Lembongan (p90)

Lazing away on a beach, riding a wave, meeting a parrot fish while snorkelling, coming face to face with a sunfish while diving in deep clear waters: these are essential experiences on Nusa Lembongan.

Touring Ubud's Rice Fields (p100)

Ribbons of green sinuously curving around hillsides crested by coconut palms and emerald patchworks blanketing the land: these are some of the vistas you'll savour as you walk Ubud's rice fields, amid Bali's sacred grain.

Bali Local Life

Insider tips to help you find the real Ba

After checking out Bali's top experiences, find out what makes this magnificent island tick. Discover the beauty of sunsets from the beaches, and savour the cultu and purely Balinese lifestyle in Ubud.

Beach Walk: Batubelig to Echo Beach (p56)

▶ Deserted beaches
▶ Isolated temples

At its busiest, Kuta Beach can feel like you've fallen into a flash mob. The same goes for Legian and even Seminyak's beaches. But head north along this seemingly limitless arc of sand from Batubelig Beach and you leave Bali's crowds behind, see seldom-visited temples and have a grand adventure. The steady pace of development means that glitzy days for this stretch of sand are just around the corner, so go now while you can still say it's your beautiful domain.

A Perfect Ubud Day (p102)

▶ Alluring shopping
▶ A cleansed body

If one Ubud is all about Balinese creativity and culture, another Ubud is much more inwardly focused. On this stroll you can get your body purged of poisons, fill it with healthy nourishment, adorn it with beauty and, bringing things full circle, feel the inspiration of Balinese dance. In fact, it is a good thing that Ubud is blessed with so many fine cafes, as otherwise you might find yourself so caught up in the pleasures of wandering its lanes that you'd forget to enjoy a break.

BY TOONMAN/GETTY IMAGES ©

Traditional kite-flying in Sanur (p89)

Ubud market

Other great ways to experience Bali like a local:

Sunset drinks on the Legian Beach sand (p32)

Seminyak sunsets at a beach bar (p42)

Seminyak shopping (p43)

Kerobokan's favourite warung (p55)

Benoa's places of worship (p80)

Sanur's expat bars (p88)

Sanur's kites (p89)

Ubud's library (p112)

Bali Day Planner

Day One

Spend your first day in Bali's tourism heart. Begin by learning to surf Kuta Beach's reliable waves at **Pro Surf School** (p26). Or learn yoga at Kerobokan's **Desa Seni** (p49). Of course you could let others do the work at the famous Seminyak spas **Prana** (p37) and **Jari Menari** (p37). No matter what, enjoy breakfast at **Biku** (p38) or **Grocer & Grind** (p40).

With the sun high overhead, hit **Kuta Beach** (p26) or **Double Six Beach** (p26). Or take shelter from the rays overhead with a little shopping in Seminyak at retailicious spots like **Lily Jean** (p43) and **Bathe** (p42) on Jl Petitenget. For lunch go local at **Warung Sulawesi** (p55) or **Warung Kolega** (p52).

Don't miss sunset drinks in the west. Buy a beer from vendors on **Legian Beach** (p32) or go more upscale at trendy **Potato Head** (p41) or at one of Seminyak's **beach shacks** (p42). Dinner calls for something great in Kerobokan: classy **Sardine** (p50) or **Sarong** (p52), or the simplicity of **Warung Sobat** (p52). Close out the night at Kuta's party that never ends starting at **Sky Garden Lounge** (p31).

Day Two

This day puts you deep into Bali's cultural soul on the island's volcanic slopes. Go early before anyone else to **Pura Luhur Batukau** (p59), where you'll find a sacred temple on the slopes of its namesake volcano. Afterwards, stop to enjoy the rice fields of **Jatiluwih** (p59) before driving east up and down the ridges of lush foothills to Ubud.

Have a healthy lunch at **Bali Buddha** (p111) or **Warung Soba** (p103). However, after the morning of Balinese culture, you may want the fabulous porky fare at **Warung Ibu Oka** (p112). After, seek serenity at **Yoga Barn** (p108) or **Bali Botanica Day Spa** (p108). Or do it yourself with a walk through **Ubud's rice fields** (p100).

One Bali experience not to be missed is a traditional dance show in Ubud. Choose your **dance performance** (p115) and watch the dancers go through their precise motions to the cacophony of the gamelan. After, fine dinner choices include **Mozaic** (p110) and **Warung Pulau Kelapa** (p110). Bedtime is early in the cool mountain air, so enjoy the symphony of insects as you shut your eyes.

Short on time?
We've arranged Bali's must-sees into these day-by-day itineraries to make sure you see the very best of the destination in the time you have available.

Day Three

☀ Using Sanur as your hub, start in Denpasar at the markets, **Pasar Badung** (p97) and **Pasar Kumbasari** (p97), when selections – and even the vendors – are the freshest. Afterwards lay low for a bit on **Sanur Beach** (p85), maybe doing a bit of swimming in the mellow waters.

☀ Have lunch at one of the places along the coast road such as **Merta Sari** (p122) and then swing up to the rice fields and lush green hills along **Sidemen Road** (p121). See if you can catch a glimpse of Bali's most important volcano, the often cloud-shrouded Gunung Agung (p121) and head south to **Semarapura** (p121) and the historically important **Taman Kertha Gosa** (p123).

☾ Back in Sanur, get in some spa time at **Jamu Traditional Spa** (p86), then hit Jl Tamblingan for some shopping at **A-Krea** (p89) for Bali-designed goods and **Ganesha Bookshop** (p89) for a recommended read. Wiggle your toes in the sand for dinner at **Bonsai Café** (p86) or go more upscale at **Massimo** (p87) or **Three Monkeys Cafe** (p86).

Day Four

☀ Spend your day south of the airport in the many-splendored but still compact Bukit Peninsula. In the morning, don't miss Jimbaran's **Fish Market** (p63), or engage with your food much more hands-on at the renowned **Bumbu Bali Cooking School** (p79). After, get soaked in the family fun of water sports at **Benoa Marine Recreation** (p80) or surf legendary breaks like **Ulu Watu** (p72).

☀ Behold beautiful Balinese art in the shady **Pasifika Museum** (p79), or follow the smart set to one of the beach coves such as **Balangan** (p69), **Bingin** (p69) and **Padang Padang** (p69). Each offers cafes on the sand and fine waters for a plunge.

☾ As the sun creates its ever-changing daily show in the west, wander through the fragrant smoke of the three main areas of Jimbaran's **seafood warungs** (p63) to find your spot for dinner or at least a sunset drink. Alternatively, head to **Pura Luhur Ulu Watu** (p71) for sunset and the **dance performance** (p75) that follows. For the best Balinese meal you'll have, consider dinner at **Bumbu Bali** (p80).

Need to Know

For more information, see Survival Guide (p145)

Currency
Rupiah (Rp)

Language
Bahasa Indonesia and Balinese

Visas
Usually 30 days, bought on arrival.

Money
ATMs in south Bali, Ubud and tourist areas. Credit cards accepted at midrange and top-end hotels and restaurants.

Mobile Phones
Local SIM cards work with any unlocked GSM phone.

Time
WIT (Central Indonesian Standard Time; GMT/UTC plus eight hours)

Plugs & Adaptors
Plugs have two round pins like Europe; electrical current is 220V. Australian and North American visitors will require plug adaptors; most electronic devices can handle 110V or 220V.

Tipping
10% for service workers is greatly appreciated.

 **Before You Go**

Your Daily Budget

Budget less than US$80
▶ Room in guesthouse/homestay less than US$50

▶ Cheap food and drink, even at fairly nice places

▶ Can survive on US$20 per day

Midrange US$80–US$220
▶ Room in midrange hotel US$50–US$150

▶ Can eat and drink virtually anywhere

▶ Can enjoy spa treatments and other luxuries

Top end over US$220
▶ Room in top-end hotel/resort over US$150

▶ Major expenses will be lavish spas

▶ Luxury boutiques await

Useful Websites

Bali Advertiser (www.baliadvertiser.biz) Bali's expat journal with insider tips and good columnists.

Bali Discovery (www.balidiscovery.com) Excellent weekly summary of news and features; hotel deals.

Lonely Planet (www.lonelyplanet.com/indonesia/bali) Destination information, hotel bookings, traveller forum and more.

Advance Planning

Three months before Book rooms during high season.

One month before Book rooms during shoulder season.

One week before Book top restaurants and spas during high season.

2 Arriving in Bali

From Bali's airport, your main choices of transport are (a) prearranged rides through your hotel or villa and (b) prepaid taxis. The former cost $10 to $50, the latter vary by destination.

✈ From Ngurah Rai Airport

Destination	Best Transport
Kuta & Legian	Taxi
Seminyak	Taxi
Kerobokan	Taxi
Sanur	Taxi
Ubud	Taxi

At the Airport

Ngurah Rai Airport Bali's Airport (DPS; listed as Denpasar or Bali on travel websites) is a chaotic construction site through 2014, when a huge new terminal building is expected to open. The arrivals area has ATMs and moneychangers. Avoid the porters. There is no duty free, unfortunate given Bali's wine and spirits prices. Accommodation services may well book you into inconvenient locations.

3 Getting Around

Taxis are the most common means of transport. However, no matter your mode, everyone is affected by the same horrific traffic in south Bali and Ubud.

🚗 Taxi

Cheap, widely available and easy to hail in south Bali. Always insist on the meter, although most will automatically use it in the daytime. Bluebird Taxis are the most reliable. In Ubud, freelance drivers charge US$2 to US$4 for rides around town.

🚗 Car & Driver

Very common for longer trips and all-day touring. Can be arranged through your hotel, and cost US$40 to US$60 per day.

🧭 Walking

The best way to get around the Kuta–Legian–Seminyak, Nusa Dua–Tanjung Benoa and Sanur areas (often on pleasant beach-front walkways) as well as Ubud.

🚗 Car

Car rentals are often arranged from streetside vendors. Cheap and adventurous, but you are at the mercy of Bali's traffic and it's very easy to get lost.

🏍 Motorbike

Cheap and easily arranged, motorbikes mean you can weave around traffic if you are a daredevil; somewhat dangerous.

🚌 Tourist Bus

Cheap air-con buses are operated by Perama Tours on a limited route that covers Kuta–Sanur–Ubud–Padangbai.

Bali Regions

Denpasar (p92)
Bali's sprawling, chaotic capital is the island's population hub. Look for museums and monuments plus vibrant shopping and eating.

Kerobokan & Echo Beach (p46)
Quickly developing area where quiet lanes lead to luxe walled-villa compounds. The beach is wilder, the waves bigger than further south.

Seminyak (p34)
Streets lined with designer boutiques and shops of every sort; oodles of good restaurants, and the beach is never far away.

Kuta & Legian (p22)
Bali's chaotic heart of mass tourism has squawking vendors and sweaty clubs all jammed in tight against a legendary beach.

Ulu Watu's Beaches

Ulu Watu & Around (p66)
Pocket-sized white-sand beaches sit in coves below cliffs. Bamboo cafes cater to surfers and their fans.

◉ Top Experiences
Hanging out at Ulu Watu's beaches

Jimbaran (p60)
A low-key bay and beach; the action is at the famous fish market and dozens of beachside grilled seafood joints.

Ubud's Rice Fields

Ubud (p98)
Bali's cultural heart is an alluring mix of creative boutiques, spas and cultural performances.

◉ Top Experiences
Touring Ubud's rice fields

Nusa Lembongan

Sanur (p82)
Combines Balinese style with a thriving expat community. The quiet beach is perfect for families too mature for Kuta.

East Bali (p118)
In the shadow of Gunung Agung, Bali's most important volcano, enjoy black-sand beaches, historic sights and impossibly green vistas.

Nusa Dua & Tanjung Benoa (p76)
Fronted by a reef-protected beach, Nusa Dua is a gated top-end resort world, while Tanjung Benoa caters to midrange groups.

Worth a Trip
◉ Top Experiences
Pura Luhur Batukau
Nusa Lembongan
Gili Trawangan

Explore
Bali

Worth a Trip

Ulu Watu (p68)
DAMIAN TURSKI/LONELY PLANET IMAGES ©

Explore

Kuta & Legian

Teeming, mad, crazy, wild, loud. Those are a few words that describe Kuta and Legian, the original tourist centre of Bali and the place that everyone either loves to hate or loves to love. Kuta's the original, with its narrow alleys *(gangs)*, hawkers, tawdry bars, cheap hotels and all-night clubs. Legian is the same, albeit for a slightly older crowd.

The Region in a Day

☀️ Start your day off taking advantage of the ever-reliable waves by learning to surf at one of the good schools such as **Pro Surf School** (p26). After a couple of hours in the water, join late-risers and all-night clubbers for an early lunch. The north end of Legian offers good choices: try either **Warung Asia** (p29) or **Warung Murah** (p29).

🌤️ In the afternoon, if time by the hotel pool doesn't divert you, head out for some serious beach action at **Kuta Beach** (p26) or **Double Six Beach** (p26). Or head indoors for some rejuvenating spa action at **Jamu Spa** (p26) or **Miracle** (p26). Don't miss **sunset drinks** (p32) from vendors on the mellow stretch of Legian Beach.

🌙 Have a leisurely Italian seafood dinner at **Mozzarella** (p28) or go basic Balinese at **Made's Warung** (p28). Now prepare for the all-night party march, the number one reason people love Kuta. Check the happy hour schedule and follow the crowds from one club to the next. Make **Sky Garden Lounge** (p31) your hub, with forays to surrounding clubs.

💗 Best of Bali

Surf Breaks
Kuta Beach (p26)

Double Six Beach (p26)

Surf Schools
Pro Surf School (p26)

Rip Curl School of Surf (p26)

Beaches
Kuta Beach (p26)

Double Six Beach (p26)

Nightlife
Sky Garden Lounge (p31)

Bounty (p32)

Pampering
Garbugar (p26)

Shopping
Surfer Girl (p33)

Rip Curl (p33)

Getting There & Around

🚗 **Taxi** Taxis from the airport, which is just south of Kuta, will cost 40,000Rp to 60,000Rp.

Walk You can easily walk all of Kuta and Legian – the beach is always the most pleasant. Jl Legian is filled with aggressive vendors.

500 m
0.25 miles

Jl Nakula

Jl Sunset

Jl Patih Jelantik

Garbugar

Miracle

5

3

8

Wave Hunter

Jl Dewi Sri

Sungai Mati

Jl Pura Puseh

Jl Majapahit

Jl Nakula

17

Jl Legian

Gang Abdi

14

LEGIAN

Jl Melasti

Jl Sahadewa

Gang Campung Mas

Jamu Spa

20

Jl Padma (Jl Yudistra)

Jl Padma Utara

Jl Arjuna (Jl Double Six)

Jl Pura Bagus Taruna
(Jl Werkudara)

15

Gang Legian Tewogah

4

16

Rip Curl School
of Surf

27

21

Jl Pantai Kuta (Kuta Beach Rd)

12

7

2

Double Six
Beach

25

Jl Imam Bonjol

Jl Blambangan

Jl Raya Kuta

BEMO
CORNER

Jl Legian

11 Memorial Wall

26

22
23
25
28

19

13

Jl Pantai Kuta

Jl Tengal Wangi

Jl Bakung Sari (Jl Singasari)

Gang Bedugul

18

Jl Lebak Bene

Naruki
Surf Shop 9

24

Poppies Gang II (Jl Batu Bolong)

KUTA

Jl Benesari

Gang Sorga

Poppies Gang I

29

10

Waterbom
Park

6 Pro Surf
School

1

Jl Pantai Kuta (Kuta Beach Rd)

Kuta
Beach

Teluk
Kuta

For reviews see

⊙ Experiences	p26
⊗ ⊗ Eating	p28
⊕ ⊕ Drinking	p31
🛍 Shopping	p33

5

6

7

8

E

D

C

B

A

Experiences

Kuta Beach
BEACH

1 ⊙ Map p24, C6

This long ribbon of golden sand and picture-perfect surf is the reason tourism started here in the first place. Always crowded with locals and tourists alike, you can get a cheap massage, drink a cold beer, gaze out to sea or ride a wave. And that's just in the morning.

Double Six Beach
BEACH

2 ⊙ Map p24, A1

This northern continuation of the Kuta–Legian strand is always one of the coolest places to hang and make new friends, whether with fellow travellers or surf-happy locals. Pick-up football games and volleyball go on all day and cheap refreshments abound. If you're feeling newly buff, come here to show off first. (Jl Arjuna)

Garbugar
MASSAGE

3 ⊙ Map p24, E4

Blind masseurs here are experts in sensing exactly where your kinks are located. It's no-frills all the way, but hard to beat for a deeply relaxing experience. (☑0361-769121; Istana Kuta Galleria, Blok OG 09; massages from 100,000Rp; ⊙10am-8pm)

Jamu Spa
SPA

4 ⊙ Map p24, B4

In serene surrounds at a resort hotel, you can enjoy indoor massage rooms that open onto a pretty garden courtyard. If you've ever wanted to be part of a fruit cocktail, here is your chance – treatments involve tropical nuts, coconuts, papayas and more, often in fragrant baths. (☑0361-752520; www.jamutraditionalspa.com; Alam Kul Kul, Jl Pantai Kuta; massages from 550,000Rp; ⊙9am-9pm)

Miracle
SPA

5 ⊙ Map p24, E4

Who can resist the name? You won't feel a bit of your acid peel here thanks to the Arctic air-con. A huge array of beauty treatments draws a loyal crowd that include many a Kuta doyen and expat. (☑0361-769019; www.miracle-clinic.com; Istana Kuta Galeria, Blok PM 1/20; massages from US$30; ⊙8.30am-8pm)

Pro Surf School
SURFING

6 ⊙ Map p24, C6

Right along the classic stretch of Kuta Beach, this well-regarded school has been getting beginners standing for years. (www.prosurfschool.com; Jl Pantai Kuta; lessons from €45)

Rip Curl School of Surf
SURFING

7 ⊙ Map p24, A1

Usually universities sell shirts with their logos, but here it's the other way round: the beachwear company spon-

Smashing down the water slide at Waterbom Park

sors a school. You can learn to surf at popular Double Six Beach; there are special courses for kids. (☎0361-735858; www.ripcurlschoolofsurf.com; Jl Arjana; lessons from 650,000Rp)

Wave Hunter BOARD RENTAL

8 Map p24, D1

Rents stand-up paddle boards, gives lessons and arranges cheap transport to and from whatever beaches have good conditions on a particular day. (www.supwavehunter.com; Jl Sunset 18X at Jl Imam Bonjol; rentals per day 250,000Rp)

Naruki Surf Shop SURFING

9 Map p24, C6

One of dozens of surf shops lining the *gangs* of Kuta, Naruki is where the friendly guys will rent you a board, fix your ding, offer advice or give you lessons. (☎0361-765772; off Poppies Gang II; ☺10am-8pm)

Waterbom Park AMUSEMENT PARK

10 Map p24, C8

Just south of Kuta, this watery amusement park covers 3.5 hectares of landscaped tropical gardens. It has assorted water slides, swimming pools and play areas, a supervised park for children under five years old, and a 'lazy river' ride. Other indulgences include the 'pleasure pool', a food court and bar, and a spa. (☎0361-755676; www.waterbom.com; Jl Kartika Plaza; adult/child US$26/16; ☺9am-6pm)

Understand
The Bali Bombings

On Saturday, 12 October 2002, two bombs exploded on Kuta's bustling Jl Legian. The first blew out the front of Paddy's Bar. A few seconds later, a far more powerful bomb obliterated the Sari Club.

The number of dead, including those unaccounted for, exceeded 200, although the exact number will probably never be known. Many injured Balinese made their way back to their villages, where, for lack of decent medical treatment, they died.

Indonesian authorities eventually laid the blame for the blasts on Jemaah Islamiyah, an Islamic terrorist group. Dozens were arrested and many were sentenced to jail, including three who received the death penalty (carried out in November 2008). But most received relatively light terms, including Abu Bakar Bashir, a radical cleric who many thought was behind the explosions (in 2011 his Bali conviction was reversed even as he was sentenced to 15 years' jail for other terrorism charges). Umar Patek, who was accused of mixing the explosives used in the bombs, was sentenced to 20 years' imprisonment in 2012.

Memorial Wall   MONUMENT

11 ⊙ Map p24, D6

Reflecting the international character of the 2002 bombings, this large memorial wall lists names of people killed in the blasts. People from many nationalities pay their respects. (Jl Legian; ⊙24hr)

Eating

Mozzarella   ITALIAN, SEAFOOD $$

12 ✕ Map p24, B2

The best of the beachfront restaurants on Legian's car-free strip, Mozzarella serves Italian fare more complex and authentic than that of its south Bali competition. Fresh fish also features; service is rather polished and you have various open-air areas for star-highlighted dining plus a more sheltered dining room. (www.mozzarella-resto.com; Maharta Bali Hotel, Jl Padma Utara Legian Kaja; meals from 60,000Rp)

Made's Warung   INDONESIAN $$

13 ✕ Map p24, D7

Made's was the original tourist warung (food stall) in Kuta. Through the years, the Westernised Indonesian menu has been much copied. Classic dishes such as *nasi campur* (rice served with side dishes) are served in an open-fronted setting that harkens back to when Kuta's tourist hot spots were lit by gas lantern. (Jl Pantai Kuta; meals from 40,000Rp)

Indo-National
WESTERN, SEAFOOD $$

14 Map p24, C3

This popular restaurant is home away from home for legions of happy fans. Grab a cold one with the rest of the crew at the bar while you take in the sweeping view of Legian's action, such as deciding which hair-plaiting style you like best. Or head back to shady and romantic tables and order the heaped-up grilled seafood platter. (Jl Padma 17; meals from 40,000Rp; 🚸)

Warung Asia
ASIAN, CAFE $

15 Map p24, B1

Look down a couple of little *gangs* for this gem: traditional Thai and Indonesian dishes served in a stylish open-air cafe, an authentic Italian espresso machine and lots of newspapers to peruse. (off Jl Arjuna & Jl Pura Bagus Taruna; meals from 30,000Rp; 📶)

Warung Murah
INDONESIAN $

16 Map p24, B1

Lunch goes swimmingly at this authentic warung specialising in seafood. An array of grilled fish awaits; if you prefer fowl over fin, the *satay ayam* is succulent *and* a bargain. It's close to Double Six Beach and is a popular hang-out through the day. Go on, have the ultimate backpacker treat, the tasty banana pancakes. (Jl Arjuna; meals from 30,000Rp; 🖊)

Saleko
INDONESIAN $

17 Map p24, C1

Just off the madness of Jl Legian, this modest open-front place draws the discerning for its simple Sumatran fare. Spicy grilled chicken and fish dare you to ladle on the volcanic sambal. Saleko is a perfect spot to start trying Indonesian fare that has not been utterly rethought for timid tourist palates. Everything is cooked halal. (Jl Nakula 4; meals from 15,000Rp)

Kori Restaurant & Bar
WESTERN, STEAKS $$

18 Map p24, D6

Kori's tables weave through a series of gardens and ponds. It has a good selection of pasta, upmarket Indonesian, burgers and more. It's ideal for a secluded rendezvous over a nonclichéd tropical drink in the

---

☑ Top Tip

Where's Double Six?

One of Southeast Asia's most famous clubs, Double Six Club, was *the* go-to party choice on Bali for years. But the island's phenomenal growth caught up with it in 2011 and its valuable beachfront real estate now hosts hotels and condos. However, the club's legacy lives on in its namesake beach and the road that gets you there, Jl Arjuna, which is still often called by its former moniker Jl Double Six.

KYLIE MCLAUGHLIN/LONELY PLANET IMAGES ©

Chilling out on Kuta Beach (p26)

flower-bedecked nooks out the back (or have one of the fabled gin and tonics). Some nights there's live acoustic music. (📞0361-758605; Poppies Gang II; meals from 70,000Rp)

Poppies Restaurant

WESTERN, INDONESIAN **$$**

19 ❌ Map p24, D7

Poppies was one of the first restaurants to be established in Kuta (Poppies Gang I is even named after it). It is popular for its lush garden setting: there are little pebbles underfoot and it feels slightly mysterious in a romantic way. The delicious food is upmarket Western and Balinese. It's just across from the gracious cottages of the same name. (📞0361-751059; Poppies Gang I; meals from 90,000Rp)

Warung Yogya

INDONESIAN **$**

20 ❌ Map p24, C3

Hidden in the heart of Legian, this simple warung is spotless and has had a recent mod makeover. It serves up hearty portions of local food for prices that would almost tempt a local. The *gado-gado* comes with a huge bowl of peanut sauce. (📞0361-750835; Jl Padma Utara; meals from 30,000Rp)

Zanzibar

WESTERN **$$**

21 ❌ Map p24, A1

Always buzzing, this popular patio fronts a busy strip at Double Six Beach. Sunset is prime time; the best views are from the swath of tables on a 2nd-floor terrace. Dishes are tasty variations on Bali menu classics like the *nasi* family and the burger bunch. If it's crowded, the many nearby competitors will also do just fine. (📞0361-733529; Jl Arjuna; meals from 50,000Rp)

Drinking

Sky Garden Lounge BAR, CLUB

22 🍷 Map p24, D6

This multilevel palace of flash flirts with height restrictions from its rooftop bar where all of Kuta twinkles around you. Look for top DJs, a ground-level cafe and paparazzi wannabes. Munchers can enjoy a long menu of bar snacks and meals, which most people pair with shots. Roam from floor to floor of this vertical playpen, posing with posers and having a blast. (www.61legian.com; Jl Legian 61; ⏱24hr)

Apache Reggae Bar CLUB

23 🍷 Map p24, D6

One of the rowdier spots in Kuta, Apache jams in locals and visitors, many of whom are on the make. The music is loud, but that pounding you feel the next day is from the free-flowing *arak* (distilled palm firewater) served in huge plastic jugs. Stumbling between here and Bounty is a Kuta tradition. (Jl Legian 146; ⏱11pm-4am)

Twice Bar MUSIC, BAR

24 🍷 Map p24, C6

From the small opening, walking into this long, narrow bar feels like entering an old carnival funhouse, the kind with black walls and the potential for a surprise a step or two away. In back, however, you'll find Kuta's best effort at an indie rock club, with all the

---

Understand
Follow the Party

Bali's trendiest clubs cluster in about a 300m radius of the top-rated Sky Garden Lounge. The distinction between drinking and clubbing is blurry at best, with one morphing into another as the night wears on (or the morning comes up). Most bars are free to enter, and often have special drink promotions and 'happy hours' that run at various intervals until after midnight. Savvy partiers follow the specials from venue to venue and enjoy a massively discounted night out (club owners count on the drink specials to lure in punters who then can't be bothered to leave). Look for cut-price drinks coupon fliers.

Bali club ambience ranges from the laid-back vibe of the surfer dives to high-concept nightclubs with long drink menus and hordes of prowling servers. Prostitutes have proliferated at some Kuta clubs.

Local Life
Sunset Drinks on the Legian Beach Sand

Bali sunsets regularly explode in stunning displays of reds, oranges and purples. Sipping a cold one while watching this free show to the beat of the surf is the top activity at 6pm. In Legian, the best place for this is the strip of beach that starts north of Jl Padma and runs to the south end of Double Six Beach. Along this car-free stretch of sand you'll find genial young local guys with simple chairs and cheap, cold beer (15,000Rp).

sweaty throngs to misbehave. It's always ladies' night here. (Jl Legian; cover from 10,000Rp; ⏲7pm-4am)

De Ja Vu   MUSIC, CAFE

27 📍 Map p24, A1

This former late-night club has morphed into the kind of hip tune-filled beach cafe that is a cliché in Byron Bay, Australia. There's still plenty of house music, but now the emphasis is more on drinking cocktails with improbable names and looking cool on the patio behind your shades. (Jl Arjuna; ⏲11am-late)

grungy – and sweaty – feel you could hope for. (Poppies Gang II; ⏲5pm-late)

Bounty   CLUB

25 📍 Map p24, D6

Set on a faux sailing boat amid a mini-mall of food and drink, the Bounty is a vast open-air disco that humps, thumps and pumps all night. Climb the blue-lit staircase and get down on the poop deck to hip-hop, techno, house and anything else the DJs come up with. Foam parties and lots of cheap shots add to the rowdiness. (Jl Legian; ⏲10pm-6am)

Mbargo   CLUB

26 📍 Map p24, D6

Throbs with the gangsta vibe, enjoyed by well-heeled, sunburnt suburbanites. Hard-edged DJs encourage the

IAN TROWER/GETTY IMAGES ©

Whiling the time away on Legian Beach

Shopping

Surfer Girl
SURFER

28 🔒 Map p24, D6

Surfer Girl's winsome logo says it all about this vast store for girls of all ages. Clothes, gear, bikinis and plenty of other stuff in every shade of bubblegum ever made. A local legend. (Jl Legian 138)

Rip Curl
SURFER

29 🔒 Map p24, C8

Cast that mopey black stuff aside and make a bit of a splash! This mothership of the surfwear giant has a huge range of beach clothes, waterwear and surfboards. (Kuta Sq)

☑ Top Tip

Shopping in Kuta & Legian

Many people spend a major part of their trip shopping. Kuta has a vast concentration of cheap places, which can be characterised by noting that the top-selling Kuta souvenir is a bottle-opener in the shape of a penis. Look for huge, flashy surf-gear emporiums on Kuta Sq and Jl Legian. As you head north along the latter into Legian, the quality of the shops improves and you start finding cute little boutiques, especially past Jl Melasti. Jl Arjuna is lined with wholesale fabric, clothing and craft stores, giving it a bazaar feel.

Explore

Seminyak

Seminyak is where you talk about designers – or claim to be one. Bali's poshest and most creative shops can be found here, starting on Jl Raya Seminyak and spreading out from the curving spine of Jl Laksmana and Jl Petitenget. This also is where you'll find scores of top restaurants from casually fun to attitudey outdoor lounges–cum–supper clubs.

The Region in a Day

☀ Start with a leisurely late breakfast at **Biku** (p38) or **Grocer & Grind** (p40). Then get yourself limbered up for the day ahead at one of Seminyak's many spas such as **Prana** (p37) or **Jari Menari** (p37). Wander over to **Seminyak Beach** (p37): feel the salty air and pause to ponder the offerings at **Pura Petitenget** (p37).

☀ Enjoy lunch at any of many casual spots that line Seminyak's restaurant row, Jl Laksmana. **Ultimo** (p39) is always popular. Now you're ready for one of Bali's highlights: shopping in Seminyak. Top options include **Theater Art Gallery** (p44) on Jl Raya Seminyak, **Lily Jean** (p43) on Jl Laksmana, **Allegra** (p43) on Jl Kayu Jati and **Bathe** (p42) on Jl Petitenget.

☾ Don't miss a spectacular sunset at trendy **Potato Head** (p41) or at one of the **beach shacks** (p42) south of Jl Abimanyu. Dinner will swamp you with choices, but it's an easy walk across the sand to **La Lucciola** (p39) or inland at **Mama San** (p39). Later, party the hours away at the somewhat refined **JP's** (p41) or the spectacle that is **Bali Jo** (p42).

🖤 Best of Bali

Beaches
Seminyak Beach (p37)

Nightlife
Potato Head (p41)

Red Carpet Champagne Bar (p41)

Bali Jo (p42)

Pampering
Prana (p37)

Jari Menari (p37)

Eating
Biku (p38)

Made's Warung II (p39)

Shopping
Bathe (p42)

Namu (p42)

Divine Diva (p42)

Getting There & Around

🚗 **Taxi** Taxis from the airport are 50,000Rp to 80,000Rp.

Walk Jl Raya Seminyak has decent walking; Jl Laksmana, Jl Petitenget and Jl Drupadi have many pedestrian perils. Beware of chasms that can cause great injury and blind corners where you are forced into traffic. If possible, opt for the beach, a quick way to Kuta and Legian.

Jl Sunset

Jl Raya Mertanadi

Jl Raya Kerobokan

Jl Pangkung Sari

Jl Oberoi (Jl Laksmana)

Jl Raya Seminyak

Jari Menari

Jl Kunti
Prana

Jl Drupadi

Jl Abimanyu (Jl Dhyana Pura)

SEMINYAK

Jl Sarinande

Seminyak
Beach

Jl Kayu Jati

Bodyworks

Jl Petitenget

Jl Pura Telagawaja

Pura
Petitenget

Jl Pantai Kaya Aya

Mana
Holistics

Kerobokan
Beach

Teluk Kuta

For reviews see

Experiences	p37
Eating	p38
Drinking	p41
Shopping	p42

500 m
0.25 miles

Experiences

Seminyak Beach
BEACH

1 ⊙ Map p36, B4

Seminyak's beach is a sandy continuation of the ribbon of sand north from Kuta and Legian. In fact the smooth, wide strip follows the breaks right round to Echo Beach in the west. The stretch of sand where Seminyak begins just north of Jl Arjuna is often less crowded than Double Six Beach to the south. The sands in front of Pura Petitenget reflect the serenity of the temple.

Pura Petitenget
TEMPLE

2 ⊙ Map p36, A2

This large complex, the scene of many ceremonies, is an important temple in a string of sea temples that stretches from Pura Luhur Ulu Watu on the Bukit Peninsula, north to Pura Tanah Lot in western Bali. The temple honours the visit of a 16th-century priest and is a fascinating place to ponder the intricacies of Balinese offerings. (Jl Pantai Kaya Aya)

Prana
SPA

3 ⊙ Map p36, E3

A palatial Moorish fantasy that is easily the most lavishly decorated spa in Bali, Prana offers everything from basic hour-long massages to facials and all manner of beauty treatments. Feel cleansed after ayurvedic treatments.

(☎0361-730840; www.thevillas.net; Jl Kunti; massages from 450,000Rp; ⊙10am-10pm)

Jari Menari
SPA

4 ⊙ Map p36, E2

Jari Menari is true to its name, which means 'dancing fingers': your body will be one happy dance floor. The all-male staff use massage techniques that emphasise rhythm. Many say this is the best place for a massage in Bali, a claim backed up by numerous awards. (☎0361-736740; Jl Raya Seminyak 47; sessions from 300,000Rp; ⊙10am-9pm)

Mana Holistics
HEALING CENTRE

5 ⊙ Map p36, A1

Rolfing, shiatsu and homeopathy are just some of the healing techniques employed at this spa-like health

☑ Top Tip

Where's Jl Oberoi?

Back in the day, roads in south Bali were often built to serve some tourist destination near the beach and took their names from same. But slowly but surely, what were once dirt trails through rice fields are getting truly Balinese names as places like Seminyak urbanise. So it is with the former Jl Oberoi (named after the luxe and highly recommended beachfront hotel), which now is called Jl Laksmana and is Seminyak's unofficial restaurant- and shop-lined main drag.

The splendour that is Prana spa (p37)

centre that emphasises natural methods. Body cleansing – inside and out – along with detox programs are designed to give you a fresh physical palette. (☎0361-318 5634; www.manaholistics.com; Jl Petitenget; treatments average 500,000Rp; ☺9am-8pm)

Bodyworks

SPA

6 ◉ Map p36, B2

Get waxed, get your hair done, get the kinks rubbed out of your joints – all this and more is on the menu at this uberpopular spa in the heart of Seminyak. The rooms are airy and everything is stress-free casual. (☎0361-733317; www.bodyworksbali.com;

Jl Kayu Jati 2; massages from 222,000Rp; ☺9am-10pm)

Eating

Biku

FUSION $$

7 🍴 Map p36, B1

Housed in an old shop that used to sell antiques, Biku retains the timeless vibe of its predecessor. The menu combines Indonesian, other Asian and Western influences; book for lunch or dinner. Dishes, from the exquisite breakfasts and the elegant local choices to Bali's best burger, are artful and delicious. There's a long list of teas and myriad refreshing cocktails. Many swoon at the sight of the cake table. (☎0361-857 0888; www.bikubali.com; Jl Petitenget; meals 40,000-120,000Rp)

Q Local Life

Follow Your Driver

The taxis and vans out front of **Ibu Mangku** (Map p36, B2; Jl Kayu Jati; meals from 20,000Rp) tell you you've found a local gem. Built of bamboo and with a serene garden out the back, this is an unexpected refuge amid the Seminyak bustle. The must-have is the superb minced-chicken satay, redolent with lemongrass and other spices.

Made's Warung II INDONESIAN $$

8 🍴 Map p36, E3

Freshly expanded, the northern branch of Made's has a buzz
many thought unlikely for such
a long-running veteran. But the
well-prepared Indonesian food is as
delicious as ever and the presentation
artful. Even the little bags of Balinese
snack crackers are a delight. You'll
need to book (or wait) in high season.
(📞0361-732130; www.madeswarung.com; Jl
Raya Seminyak; meals 40,000-160,000Rp)

Mama San FUSION $$

9 🍴 Map p36, D2

All the action is on the 2nd floor of
this buzzy warehouse-sized restaurant right on the edge of Seminyak
and Sunset Roads. A long cocktail list
provides liquid balm for the mojito
set and has lots of tropical-flavoured
pours. The menu emphasises small
dishes from across Southeast Asia.
(📞0361-730436; www.mamasanbali.com;
Jl Raya Kerobokan 135; meals 60,000-
120,000Rp)

La Lucciola FUSION $$$

10 🍴 Map p36, A2

A sleek beachside restaurant with
good views from the 2nd-floor tables
across a lovely lawn and sand to the
surf. The bar is big with sunset-
watchers, although most then move
on to dinner. The menu is a creative
melange of international fare with
an Italian flair. (📞0361-730838; Jl Pantai
Kaya Aya; meals from 120,000Rp)

Hu'u FUSION $$$

11 🍴 Map p36, A1

Oodles of little tea candles provide
a romantic glow at night for tables
under the stars. There's steak, seafood
and a good selection of vegetarian
dishes plus interesting takes on local
dishes. Service is polished; late in the
evening Hu'u takes on a nightclub
vibe. (📞0361-736443; www.huubali.com;
Jl Pantai Kaya Aya; meals from 80,000Rp;
⏰11am-2am)

Ultimo ITALIAN $$

12 🍴 Map p36, C2

It's simple to count your way to
dining joy at this vast and always
popular restaurant in a part of Seminyak as thick as a risotto with eateries.
Choose a table overlooking the street
action, out back in one of the gardens,
or inside. Ponder the surprisingly authentic menu and then let the army of
servers take charge. (www.balinesia.co.id;
Jl Laksmana 104; meals 60,000-220,000Rp)

Sate Bali INDONESIAN $$

13 🍴 Map p36, B3

Ignoring the strip-mall location, enjoy
traditional Balinese dishes at this small
cafe run by chef Nyoman Sudiyasa
(who also has a cooking school here).
The *rijsttafel* (multicourse menu) is a
symphony of tastes, including the addictive *babi kecap* (pork in a sweet soy

Beachfront fun at Ku De Ta

sauce) and *tum bebek* (minced duck in banana leaf). (Jl Laksmana; meals from 90,000Rp; ⊙11am-10pm)

Grocer & Grind   CAFE, DELI $$

14 Map p36, B2

Keep your vistas limited and you might think you're just at a sleek Sydney cafe, but look around and you're unmistakeably in Bali, albeit one of the trendiest bits. Classic sandwiches, salads and big breakfasts issue forth from the kitchen. Eat in the open air or choose air-con tables in the deli area. (Jl Kayu Jati 3X; meals from 40,000Rp; 🛜)

Bali Deli   SUPERMARKET $$

15 Map p36, E3

Almost at Jl Sunset, the lavish deli counter at this market is loaded with imported cheeses, meats and baked goods. This is the place to come for above-average wines for the villa or to prepare a killer picnic. (Jl Kunti 117X)

Earth Cafe   HEALTH FOOD $

16 Map p36, C2

The good vibes are organic at this vegetarian cafe and store amid the upmarket retail ghetto of Seminyak. Choose from creative salads, sandwiches or wholegrain vegan goodies. A retail section sells healthful potions and lotions. While perusing the bookshelves, don't get ahead of yourself in the colonic irrigation section. (Jl Laksmana; meals from 40,000Rp; ✈)

Drinking

Potato Head
CLUB

17 Map p36, A1

The newest beach club in Seminyak is also the grooviest. Wander up off the sand or follow a long drive off the main road and you'll discover a truly captivating creation on a grand scale. The clever design is striking and you'll find much to amuse, from an enticing pool to a cafe and a swanky restaurant. (Jl Petitenget)

Mano
CAFE

18 Map p36, A2

Tucked away behind Pura Petitenget, this basic beachside cafe overlooks a lovely and uncrowded swath of sand in otherwise busy Seminyak. Escape the crowds and fake glam elsewhere for a cold one here. (Petitenget Beach)

Red Carpet Champagne Bar
CAFE, BAR

19 Map p36, D2

The closest most will come to posing for paparazzi is at this over-the-top glam bar on Seminyak's couture strip. Waltz the red carpet and toss back a few namesake flutes while contemplating a raw oyster and displays of frilly frocks. It's open to the street (but

elevated dahling) so you can observe the rabble. (Jl Laksmana 42)

JP's
CAFE, BAR

20 Map p36, D4

From a modest open front to the street, JP's unfolds in a series of rooms that add up to a quite large U-shaped lounge with a variety of areas, from dining to dancing to chilling, which can suit most moods. Live music can be Cuban, local rock or even a well-known jazz flautist. (www.jps-warungclub.com; Jl Abimanyu)

Ku De Ta
CLUB

21 Map p36, B3

Ku De Ta teems with Bali's beautiful people (including those whose status is purely aspirational). Scenesters perfect their 'bored' look over drinks during the day, gazing at the fine stretch of surf right out the back. Sunset brings out crowds, who snatch a cigar at the bar or dine on eclectic fare at tables. The music throbs with increasing intensity through the night. (Jl Laksmana; ☺7am-1am)

Shopping

Bathe   COSMETICS, HOMEWARES

22 🔒 Map p36, B1

Double-down on your villa's romance with the handmade candles and bath salts at this shop that evokes the feel of a 19th-century French dispensary. You can't help but smile at the tub filled with rubber ducks. (Jl Petitenget 100X)

🔍 Local Life
Seminyak Sunsets at a Beach Bar

At the beach end of Jl Abimanyu in Seminyak you have a choice: turn right for beach bars and lounges, or turn left for a much more purely Balinese experience. You'll discover mock-Moorish affairs with oodles of huge pillows for lounging, and all manner of simple bars lining the path along the sand. It's all more flash than the local guys selling beers from coolers in Legian (p32) but just as much fun. Often there's even live music as the light fades.

🔍 Local Life
Gay Seminyak

A stretch of Seminyak's Jl Abimanyu is the island's defacto gay bastion. A strip of small bars and clubs are filled with revellers most nights, with the crowds more mixed at some than others. **Obsession** (Map p36, D4; Jl Abimanyu; ☺6pm-2am) offers 'global music' at a rather intimate venue. Latin, blues, soul and more get bodies grooving through the night.

Bali Jo (Map p36, D4; Jl Abimanyu; ☺8pm-3am) is simply fun – albeit with falsies. Drag queens rock the house and the flamboyant shows draw crowds both inside and watching from out on the street.

Namu   CLOTHING

23 🔒 Map p36, A1

Designer Paola Zancanaro creates comfy and casual resortwear for men and women that doesn't take a holiday from style. The fabrics are lusciously tactile; many hand-painted silk. (Jl Petitenget)

Divine Diva   CLOTHING

24 🔒 Map p36, D2

It's like a Dove soap commercial for real women in this shop, filled with Bali-made breezy styles for larger figures. One customer told us: 'It's the essence of agelessness.' (Jl Laksmana 1A)

Biasa
CLOTHING

25 🔒 Map p36, E4

This is Bali-based designer Su-
sanna Perini's premier shop. Her
line of tropicalwear for men and
women combines cottons, silks and
embroidery. The results are elegant
and would pass for resortwear any
place posh. (www.biasabali.com; Jl Raya
Seminyak 36)

Blue Glue
BIKINIS

26 🔒 Map p36, D2

How best to show off your form on
the see-and-be-seen stretches of Bali
beach, especially in uberhip Seminyak? Try one of these trendy Bali-
designed bathing suits at this flash
new boutique. (Jl Raya Kerobokan)

Lily Jean
CLOTHING

27 🔒 Map p36, C2

Saucy knickers underpin sexy women's
clothing that both dares and flirts;
most is Bali-made. This popular shop
has flash new digs in fashion's ground
zero. (Jl Laksmana)

Street Dogs
ACCESSORIES

28 🔒 Map p36, D2

Bracelets made with shells and resin
as well as recycled brass demand im-
mediate wearing. (Jl Laksmana 60)

Allegra
WOMEN'S CLOTHING

29 🔒 Map p36, B2

Clothes that are very feminine yet also
girly and quirky. The owner/designer
is from Australia and this is a top spot
on the booming strip of Jl Kayu Jati.
(Jl Kayu Jati)

Inti
WOMEN'S CLOTHING

30 🔒 Map p36, D2

Shoppers tired of pawing through
racks of size-2 clothes will sigh with
relief at this shop filled with resortwear aimed at mature women. (Jl Raya
Seminyak 11)

Local Life
Seminyak Shopping

The shopping scene here is constantly changing: new boutiques
appear, old ones vanish, some
change into something else while
others move up the food chain.
Seminyak shops could occupy days
of your holiday. Designer boutiques,
funky stores, slick galleries, wholesale emporiums and family-run
workshops are just some of the
choices.

The interesting retail action
picks up going north from the junction with Jl Arjuna where Jl Legian
morphs into Jl Raya Seminyak. The
hunt gets especially ripe north of
Jl Abimanyu. Shopping peaks on Jl
Laksmana, Jl Kayu Jati and on into
Kerobokan along Jl Petitenget.

Homewares, Seminyak style

Theater Art Gallery PUPPETS

31 Map p36, E4

Specialises in vintage and reproduction puppets used in traditional Balinese theatre. Just browsing the animated faces peering back at you is a delight. (Jl Raya Seminyak)

Ashitaba WOVEN BASKETS

32 Map p36, E3

Tenganan, the Aga village of east Bali, produces the intricate and beautiful rattan items sold here. Containers, bowls, purses and more (from US$5) display the very fine weaving. (Jl Raya Seminyak 6)

Milo's CLOTHING

33 Map p36, B2

The legendary local designer of silk finery has followed the hordes to designer row and opened this lavish shop. Look for batik-bearing, eye-popping orchid patterns. (www.milos-bali.com; Jl Laksmana)

Paul Ropp CLOTHING

34 Map p36, D2

The elegant main shop for one of Bali's premier high-end fashion designers. Most goods are made just a few kilometres away in the hills above Denpasar. And what goods they are – rich silks and cottons, vivid to the point of gaudy, with hints of

Ropp's roots in the tie-dyed 1960s.
(www.paulropp.com; Jl Laksmana)

Samsara   CLOTHING

35 🔒 Map p36, E3

True Balinese-made textiles are
increasingly rare as production moves
to Java and other places with cheaper
labour. But the local family behind
this tidy shop still source hand-
painted Batik for a range of exquisite
casualwear. (Jl Raya Seminyak)

Periplus   BOOKS

36 🔒 Map p36, B2

A large outlet of the island-wide chain
of lavishly fitted bookshops. Besides
enough design books to have you
fitting out even your garage with 'Bali
Style', there are bestsellers, magazines
and newspapers. (Seminyak Sq)

☑ Top Tip

Wrong Number?

Bali's landline phone numbers
(those with area codes that include 0361, across the south and
Ubud) are being changed on an
ongoing basis through 2014. To
accommodate increased demand
for lines, a digit is being added
to the start of the existing six- or
seven-digit phone number. So
0361-761 xxxx might become
0361-4761 xxxx. The schedule and
plans for the new numbers change
regularly, but usually you'll hear a
recording first in Bahasa Indonesian and then in English telling you
what digit to add to the changed
number.

Explore

Kerobokan
& Echo Beach

Kerobokan can rightly be called Seminyak North. Jl Petitenget seam-lessly links the pair and, like its southern neighbour, Kerobokan has an ever more alluring collection of shops and some of Bali's very best restaurants. This is also ground zero for private villa rentals, with walled compounds stretching west with the coast past villa-dotted Canggu to the rugged surf and idyll pleasures of Echo Beach.

The Region in a Day

☀ Start your day off with you! Try some yoga at **Desa Seni** (p49) or a new look at **Amo Beauty Spa** (p49). Go for an invigorating ride on the beach with a horse from **Umalas Stables** (p50). Or just lighten your pocketbook while filling the carry-on at any of many fine housewares stores such as **Hobo** (p55). (Save money *and* space at the kid-friendly **JJ Bali Button** (p54).)

☀ Kerobokan has a number of simple warungs that showcase Indonesian foods in a setting visitors will enjoy; try **Warung Sulawesi** (p55) or **Warung Kolega** (p52). For the afternoon, find your perfect spot of sand at the ever-more-popular **Batubelig Beach** (p49) or **Echo Beach** (p49), where you'll find sunbed, and drink vendors. Or go for one of the much-less-visited stretches of sand between these two.

☾ Look for a venue that grabs your fancy for sunset views at Batubelig Beach, just west of Kerobokan. Then don a frilly frock and choose from some of Bali's best drinking and dining at **Sardine** (p50) or **Sarong** (p52), or go down and tasty at **Warung Sobat** (p52).

 Best of Bali

Surf Breaks
Echo Beach (p49)

Beaches
Batubelig Beach (p49)

Echo Beach (p49)

Pampering
Desa Seni (p49)

Eating
Sardine (p50)

Sarong (p52)

Waroeng Bonita (p52)

Warung Sobat (p52)

Warung Sulawesi (p55)

Shopping
JJ Bali Button (p54)

Hobo (p55)

Getting There & Around

🚗 **Taxi** Taxis from the airport will cost 70,000Rp to 120,000Rp.

The Kerobokan, Canggu and Echo Beach area is quite spread out. Renting a scooter, taking a taxi or getting rides from your villa driver (if you have one) will be necessary. Echo Beach has a taxi stand.

SEMER

KUWUM

6 Umalas Stables

18
20 16
Jl Raya Kerobokan
19

12 8

UMALA KANGIN

11

Jl Petitenget

Spa 5 9
Bonita Amo
4 Beauty
Spa

KEROBOKAN

17

10

Batubelig
Beach
1

Kerobokan
Beach

CANGGU

15
Sukyf Arch & Art 7

Desa
Seni
3

Jl Pantai Berawa

Jl Pamelisan Agung

Jl Nelayan

Jl Pantai Batu Bolong

Jl Subak Catur

Teluk
Kuta

N
0 1 km
0 0.5 miles

Echo
Beach
2
14
13

For reviews see

●	Experiences	p49
✗	Eating	p50
●	Drinking	p54
●	Shopping	p54

Experiences

Batubelig Beach
BEACH

1 ◎ Map p48, C4

Part of south Bali's famed beach, Batubelig has pounding surf, long stretches of usually uncrowded sand and one or two simple beach cafes. New developments such as the flash W Hotel to the south and an influx of upscale restaurants mean that the vibe will soon be action-packed.

Echo Beach
BEACH

2 ◎ Map p48, A1

Cafes from basic to vaunted front some of Bali's most reliable surf breaks. Enjoy a beverage while critiquing the board-riders, or take the plunge yourself. If it seems a might crowded right at the cafes, walk 200m along the beach in either direction for solitude.

Desa Seni
YOGA

3 ◎ Map p48, C2

Desa Seni bills itself as a 'village resort' and comprises classic wooden homes up to 220 years old brought to the site from across Indonesia and turned into luxurious quarters. However, it is also renowned for its wide variety of yoga classes, which are offered daily. (☏0361-844 6392; www.desaseni.com; Jl Kayu Putih 13; classes from 120,000Rp; ⊙varies)

Amo Beauty Spa
SPA

4 ◎ Map p48, D4

With some of Asia's top models lounging about it feels like you've stepped into the studios of *Vogue*. Besides massages, other services range from hair care to pedicures and unisex waxing. (☏0361-275 3337; www.amospa.com; 100 Jl Petitenget; massage from 180,000Rp; ⊙9am-9pm)

Spa Bonita
SPA

5 ◎ Map p48, D4

Part of the delightful Waroeng Bonita, this male-oriented spa has a range of services in a simple, elegant setting. (☏0361-731918; www.bonitabali.com; Jl Petitenget 2000X; massages from 100,000Rp; ⊙9am-9pm)

☑ Top Tip

Avoiding Tanah Lot

Just west of Echo Beach, Pura Tanah Lot is a heavily touristed temple right on the ocean. Although picturesque, much of its structure – which sits on rocks amid the surf – is of very recent construction. The scores of souvenir-sellers jamming the site coupled with the nightmarish traffic jams for sunset-viewing make a visit anything but serene. For a much more pleasant experience, opt for Pura Ulu Watu instead.

SONNY TUMBELAKA/AFP/GETTY IMAGES ©

Making an offering

Umalas Stables
HORSE RIDING

6 Map p48, E2

Pick your pony in this elegant compound set among the paddies. It has a stable of 30 horses and ponies, and offers 30-minute rice-field tours and two- and three-hour beach rides (a trip highlight for many tourists). Lessons for beginner to advanced equestrians in dressage and show jumping can also be arranged. (0361-731402; www.balionhorse.com; Jl Lestari 9X; beach rides from US$72)

Sukyf Arch & Art
GALLERY

7 Map p48, C2

Some of Bali's best artists show in this attractive gallery in the middle of ever-expanding Canggu, not far from the Canggu Club. (www.sukyf.com; Jl Subak Sari 4; 10am-6pm)

Eating

Sardine
SEAFOOD $$$

8 Map p48, E3

Seafood fresh from the famous Jimbaran market is the star at this elegant yet intimate, casual yet stylish restaurant in a beautiful bamboo pavilion. Open-air tables overlook a private rice field that is patrolled by Sardine's own flock of ducks. The inventive bar is a must. The menu changes to reflect what's fresh. Booking is vital. (0361-738202;

Understand

The Villa Life

Like temple offerings after a ceremony, villas can be found across south Bali, with the greatest concentration in Kerobokan and Canggu. They're often built in the middle of rice paddies, seemingly overnight. The villa boom has been quite controversial for environmental, aesthetic and economic reasons (many skip collecting government taxes from guests).

Villas can be bacchanal retreats for groups of friends who share multiple bedrooms set around a pool. Others are smaller, more intimate and part of larger developments. Expect a private garden and pool (which can range in size from plunge to substantial), a kitchen (you can usually arrange for a cook if you want to eat in your compound), air-con bedroom(s) and an open-air common space.

Also potentially included are your own staff (cook, driver, cleaner) or at least staff shared with a few units, lush grounds, private beachfront, isolation (which can be good or bad, eg Canggu can be isolated by traffic jams) and wi-fi.

After dark some villa walls hide surprises. On any night in Kerobokan and Canggu there are a few private parties going on that are a bit bigger than your average kegger in a backyard. Many feature top DJs and an attitude-heavy list of visiting (self-professed) celebrities and the like. Getting an invite to one of these soirees is rather elusive, although on occasion uninvited guests turn up in the form of police, who invariably make a few arrests for drugs.

Renting a Villa

Rates range from under US$200 per night for a modest villa to US$1200 per night and beyond for your own tropical estate. There are often deals, especially in the low season, and several couples sharing can make something grand affordable. Agents include **Bali Discovery** ([☎]0361-286283; www.balidiscovery.com), **Bali Private Villas** ([☎]0361-316 6455; www.baliprivatevillas.com), **Bali Tropical Villas** ([☎]0361-732083; www.bali-tropical-villas.com) and **Bali Ultimate Villas** ([☎]0361-8571658; www.baliultimatevillas.com).

Some things to keep in mind and ask about when renting a villa: how far is the villa from the beach and stores? Is a driver or car service included? If there is a cook, is food included? Is laundry included?

www.sardinebali.com; Jl Petitenget 21; meals US$15-35; ⊗closed Mon)

Sarong   FUSION $$

9 ⊗ Map p48, D4

The food is almost as magical as the setting at this top-end, high-concept restaurant. Largely open to the evening breezes, the dining room has plush furniture and gleaming place settings that twinkle in the candle-light. But opt for tables out the back where you can let the stars do the twinkling. The food spans the globe; small plates are popular with those wishing to pace an evening enjoying the commodious bar. (☎0361-737809; www.sarongbali.com; Jl Petitenget 19X; meals US$10-30; ⊗noon-10pm)

Waroeng Bonita   INDONESIAN $$

Balinese dishes such as *ikan rica-rica* (fresh fish in a spicy green-chilli sauce) are the specialities at this cute little place (see 5 ⊙ Map p48, D4) with tables set out under the trees. There's a breezy style that attracts people every night, but on certain nights Bonita positively heaves because of the drag shows starring everyone from visiting queens to the busboy. (www.bonitabali.com; Jl Petitenget 2000X; meals 70,000-200,000Rp)

Warung Sobat   SEAFOOD $

10 ⊗ Map p48, D3

Set in a sort of bungalow-style brick courtyard, this old-fashioned restaurant (with bargain prices) excels at fresh Balinese seafood with an Italian accent (lots of garlic!). First-time visitors feel like they've made a discovery, and if you have the sensational lobster platter (a bargain at 350,000Rp for two; order in advance), you will too. Book. (Jl Batubelig 11; meals 50,000-150,000Rp)

Warung Kolega   INDONESIAN $

11 ⊗ Map p48, D4

A Javanese halal classic. Choose your rice (we prefer the fragrant yellow), then pick from a delectable array that includes tempeh in sweet chilli sauce, *sambal terung* (spicy eggplant), *ikan sambal* (spicy grilled fish) and other daily specials. (Jl Petitenget; meals 25,000Rp; ⊗11am-3pm)

Cafe Degan   ASIAN $$

12 ⊗ Map p48, E3

The young couple running this cultured little warung have created a winner. The menu veers towards Indonesian but overall features dishes from the region you don't often find, such as *daging sambal hijau* (spicy beef with green chillies). A small air-con bakery has an array of delectables for dessert. (Jl Petitenget 9; meals 90,000-160,000Rp)

Beach House   CAFE $$

13 ⊗ Map p48, A1

Face the Echo Beach waves from stylish loungers or chill on a variety of couches and picnic tables. Enjoy the

MOTH/DREAMSTIME.COM ©

Balinese seafood curry

menu of breakfasts, salads, grilled fare and tasty dishes such as calamari with aioli. On Sunday nights it offers a hugely popular outdoor barbecue. (Jl Pura Batu Mejan; dishes 30,000-100,000Rp; 🛜)

Mandira Cafe   CAFE $

14 🍴 Map p48, A1

Although Echo Beach is rapidly going upscale, this classic surfers' dive has battered picnic tables with front-row seats for surfing action. Quaff a cheap Bintang while you Instagram the best action out on the breaks. The timeless menu includes jaffles, banana pancakes, club sandwiches and smoothies. (Jl Pura Batu Mejan; meals 25,000-50,000Rp; 🛜)

Trattoria   ITALIAN $$

15 🍴 Map p48, C2

The latest outlet of this Seminyak original anchors a collection of restaurants around a pleasant courtyard in the centre of Canggu. Trattoria has a large menu of classic Italian fare and pizzas; other adjoining venues include sushi and a fine coffee house. (Jl Pantai Berawa; meals 90,000-160,000Rp)

Fruit Market   MARKET $

16 🍴 Map p48, E3

Bali's numerous climate zones (hot and humid near the ocean, cool and dry up the volcano slopes) mean that pretty much any fruit or vegetable can be grown within the island's small confines. Look for the full range at the many vendor tables here, including oddball fruits you'll have never seen before (try a nubby mangosteen). (cnr Jl Raya Kerobokan & Jl Gunung Tangkuban Perahu; ⊙7am-7pm)

Drinking

Naughty Nuri's   CAFE

17 🕹 Map p48, D3

This large Kerobokan cafe avoids the over-hype of the Ubud original by delivering solid fare and the trademark kick-ass martinis. As you'd expect, ribs are grilling on open coals up front, but whereas the main location often runs

short of tables, this commodious outpost nearly always has room for you to enjoy a cold Bintang or something more fun. (Jl Batubelig 41)

Shopping

JJ Bali Button   BUTTONS

18 🔒 Map p48, E3

Zillions of beads and buttons made from shells, plastic, metal and more are displayed in what at first looks like a candy store. Elaborately carved wooden buttons are 700Rp. Wander around the nearby streets, especially Jl Raya Mertanadi, for an everchanging line-up of homeware shops,

STEPHANE VICTOR/LONELY PLANET IMAGES ©

Naughty Nuri's ribs

many of them more factory than showroom. (Jl Gunung Tangkuban Perahu)

Hobo   HOMEWARES

19 🔒 Map p48, E4

Elegance mixes with quirky at this enticing shop filled with gifts and housewares, most of which can slip right into your carry-on bag. This part of Jl Raya Kerobokan abounds in shops worth browsing. (Jl Raya Kerobokan)

Lio   HOMEWARES

20 🔒 Map p48, E3

A minor empire with shops all along this stretch of road. Housewares, rattan antiques, reproductions and more. (Jl Raya Kerobokan)

Q Local Life

Kerobokan's Favourite Warung

Although seemingly upscale, Kerobokan is blessed with many a fine place for a local meal. One of the very favourites is **Warung Sulawesi** (Map p48, D3; Jl Petitenget; meals from 25,000Rp; ☉11am-6pm). Here you'll find a table in a quiet family compound and enjoy fresh Balinese and Indonesian food served in classic warung style. Choose a rice, then pick from a captivating array of dishes that are always at their peak at noon. The long beans – yum!

Local Life
Beach Walk: Batubelig to Echo Beach

Getting There

🚗 **Taxi** Getting to Batubelig is easy by cab. Echo Beach has its own taxi drivers so getting a ride back is also easy.

Walking the beach, it's only 4km from Batubelig Beach to Echo Beach, compared with a long circuitous drive inland. You'll cover long stretches of empty sand and ford a few streams with only the roar of the surf for company. A few villages, temples, expat villas and simple cafes provide interest away from the water. Be aware you'll get wet on this walk; have waterproof bags for everything.

❶ Batubelig Beach

Start this walk at one of the beach bars and cafes along Batubelig Beach. Get your fluids in for an adventure that can take anywhere from an hour to half a day depending on your whim. Look northwest along the beach and you can see the developments at Echo Beach in the distance.

❷ Water Crossing

The biggest obstacle on this entire walk is only about 500m from the start. The river and lagoon here flow into the ocean, often at a depth of 1m but at times not at all. However, after rains it may be much deeper and you'll decide not to swim the current: in this case, take the cool little footbridge over the lagoon to **Warung Agung Kayu Putih** (Jl Pura Kayu Putih), which has a basic menu, good views and a phone for a taxi.

❸ Berewa Beach

Greyish Berewa Beach, secluded among rice fields and villas, is about 2km up the sand from Seminyak (where you can also begin this walk). There are a couple of surfer cafes by the pounding sea; the grey volcanic sand here slopes steeply into foaming water. Look on the sand's edge for the vast **Marabito Art Villa**, a private estate that's an architectural wonder.

❹ Pantai Prancak

Almost 1km further on you'll come to another (shallow) water crossing that also marks the large complex of **Pura Dalem Prancak**. A vendor or two may offer drinks on Pantai Prancak; turn around facing the way you've come and you can see the sweep of the beach all the way to the airport.

❺ Pantai Nelayan

A collection of fishing boats and huts marks this very mellow stretch of sand that lacks easy access to villa-land just inland.

❻ Pantai Batu Bolong

Sometimes called Canggu Beach, Pantai Batu Bolong boasts the large **Pura Batumejan** complex with a striking pagoda-like temple. There are surfboard rentals and some groovy cafes. About 200m further on there's a slightly upscale beach vendor with comfy loungers for rent and drinks.

❼ Echo Beach

Construction all along the shore means you've reached Echo Beach, where you can reward yourself for your adventurous walk at the many cafes. A growing flock of stores means you can replace any clothes that are drenched beyond repair. Otherwise, take your camera out of its waterproof bag and nab shots of the popular surf break.

❽ Pererenan Beach

Yet to be found by the right developer, Pererenan Beach is for you if you want your sand windswept and your waves unridden. It's an easy 300m further on from Echo Beach by sand and rock formations. There are a couple of good cafes here that don't have the mobs of Echo Beach.

Top Experiences
Feeling Spiritual at Pura Luhur Batukau

Getting There

🚗 **Car** You'll need to charter a car and driver for the day. Getting here from south Bali can take one to two hours, depending on traffic.

One of the island's holiest and most underrated temples, Pura Luhur Batukau makes for an excellent day trip and is the most spiritual temple you can easily visit. It is surrounded by forest, the atmosphere is cool and misty; the chants of priests are backed by birds singing. The temple is near the base of Gunung Batukau, the island's second-highest mountain (2276m) and the third of Bali's three major volcanoes. Nearby, you can drive through the lushly iconic Jatiluwih rice fields.

The temple grounds at Pura Luhur Batukau

Don't Miss

Pura Luhur Batukau

Within the temple complex look for the seven-roofed *meru* dedicated to Maha Dewa, the mountain's guardian spirit, as well as shrines for Bratan, Buyan and Tamblingan Lakes. The main *meru* in the inner courtyard have little doors shielding small ceremonial items. It's impossible to ignore the deeply spiritual mood.

Facing the temple, take a short walk around to the left to see a small white-water stream where the air resonates with tumbling water. Get here early for the best chance of seeing the dark and foreboding slopes of the volcano.

Gunung Batukau

From Pura Luhur Batukau you can climb Gunung Batukau. To trek to the top of the 2276m peak, you'll need a guide, which can be arranged at the temple. Expect to pay 1,200,000Rp (for two people) for an arduous journey that will take at least seven hours one way. The rewards are amazing views alternating with thick dripping jungle.

Jatiluwih Rice Fields

At Jatiluwih, which means 'truly marvellous', you will be rewarded with vistas of centuries-old rice terraces that exhaust your ability to describe green. Emerald ribbons curve around the hillsides, stepping back as they climb to the blue sky.

The terraces are emblematic of Bali's ancient rice-growing culture. Stop along the narrow, twisting 18km road and follow the water as it runs through channels and bamboo pipes from one plot to the next.

Admission to Pura Batukau: 10,000Rp donation

☑ Top Tips

▸ Sashes and sarongs are provided.

▸ Admire the many forms of offerings from a few flower petals in a banana leaf to vastly elaborate affairs that can feed many gods.

▸ A two-hour mini-jaunt up Batukau costs 300,000Rp.

▸ There is a road toll for Jatiluwih visitors (10,000Rp per person, plus 5000Rp per car).

▸ Much of the rice you'll see is traditional, rather than the hybrid versions grown elsewhere on the island. Look for heavy short husks of red rice.

✗ Take a Break

There are a couple of simple cafes for refreshments along the Jatiluwih drive. They are nothing fancy, but you're there for the views.

Explore

Jimbaran

For many, Jimbaran means a wonderful grilled seafood dinner over-looking the serene bay from tables on the sand. By day, Jimbaran has two markets that bustle with business as Bali's rich stocks of fish, fruits and vegetables are bought and sold. The sweeping crescent of sand fronting the bay is a fine alternative to venturing further along the Bukit Peninsula.

The Region in a Day

Morning in Jimbaran comes very early, but waking with the sun will be rewarded when you visit the frenetic world of the **Fish Market** (p63) as well as the fruit and vegetable wonderland that is the **Morning Market** (p63). For a pause, you might try a cafe in one of the resorts that are discreetly set back from the beach.

Your afternoon should be all about Jimbaran's excellent **beach** (p63). Stroll its 4km and find a good shady spot to relax on a rented sun lounger. Despite rumours of development plans, the area is not overwhelmed yet with hotels and resorts so you won't find the sands crowded.

As the sun creates its spectacular vermillion theatrics in the west, wander through the fragrant smoke of the three main areas of seafood warungs to find your spot for dinner. The fish is always fresh from the market and you can choose from what's on offer in huge tanks and beds of ice before it goes on the flaming coconut-shell-fuelled grills.

 Best of Bali

Eating
Teba Mega Cafe (p63)

Getting There & Around

Taxi Taxis from Kuta will cost 50,000Rp; from Seminyak about 80,000Rp. Traffic on the main road past the airport can get clogged, leading to very long delays.

Walk You can easily walk Jimbaran's beach to browse the seafood warungs and market.

Fish Market **2**

Jl Pantai Kedongganan

⌃ 0 _____ 500 m
Ⓝ 0 _____ 0.25 miles

For reviews see
⊙ Experiences	p63
✕ Eating	p63
🔒 Shopping	p65

Northern Seafood Warung **7**

KEDONGANAN

Jl Pantai Jimbaran

Jl Ulu Watu

Jl Ngurah Rai Bypass

Teluk Jimbaran

Middle Seafood Warung

Pura Ulun Siwi

Jl Pemelisan Agung **4** ⊙ **3** Morning Market

Jl Ulunsiwi

6 ✕

Jimbaran Beach ⊙**1**

Jl Yoga Perkanti

Southern Seafood Warung

JIMBARAN

5 ✕

Jl Bukit Permai

Jl Ulu Watu II

8 🔒

Experiences

Jimbaran Beach
BEACH

1 Map p62, B4

One of Bali's very best beaches, Jimbaran's 4km-long arc of sand fronts its namesake bay. The sand is mostly very clean and there is no shortage of places to get a snack, a drink, a seafood dinner or rent a sun lounger. The bay keeps the surf mellower than at Kuta, although you can still get breaks that are fun for body surfing.

Fish Market
FISH MARKET

2 Map p62, B1

A popular morning stop on Bukit Peninsula ambles is this smelly, lively and frenetic fish market – just watch where you step. Brightly painted boats bob along the shore while huge cases of everything from small sardines to fearsome langoustines are hawked. The action is fast and furi-

---

✅ Top Tip

Surfing

Jimbaran is a good place to access the very popular surf breaks off the airport. Head up the beach looking for a fishing boat (if you have a board, skippers will find you) and negotiate to be taken out to the breaks. Prices are very negotiable: 50,000Rp for a one-way trip is a good place to start.

---

ous; for more see p64. (Jimbaran Beach; ⏱6am-3pm)

Morning Market
FOOD MARKET

3 Map p62, C3

This is one of the best markets in Bali for a visit because (a) it's compact so you can see a lot without wandering forever (b) local chefs swear by the quality of the fruits and vegetables (ever seen a cabbage that big?) and (c) they're used to tourists tromping about. (Jl Ulu Watu; ⏱6am-noon)

Pura Ulun Siwi
TEMPLE

4 Map p62, C3

Across from the morning market, this ebony-hued temple from the 18th century is a snoozy place until it explodes with life, offerings, incense and more on a holy day. (Jl Ulu Watu)

Eating

Teba Mega Cafe
SEAFOOD $$

5 Map p62, B5

The southern seafood warungs are a compact collection at the very south end of the beach. There's a parking area off Jl Bukit Permai, and the beach here is well groomed with nice trees. Call for transport. Teba is the favourite of many long-term Bali expats; its seafood platters are just a smidge better than the rest. (off Jl Bukit Permai; meals 80,000-200,000Rp)

Understand
Seafood in Jimbaran

From Jimabaran's beautiful beach you'll see a constant stream of fishing boats coming and going from the bustle and scrum of the **Jimbaran Fish Market** (p63), where Bali's restaurants purchase the fish caught in the local waters.

Pascal Chevillot, owner of Kerobokan's award-winning Sardine seafood restaurant, is there many mornings. 'New seafood arrives constantly as boats pull up to the beach. You know you'll find certain things like excellent shellfish all the time, but it's also an adventure as what's caught changes daily.'

Among the warren of shouting vendors, slippery, slimy footing and box-carrying porters elbowing past, Chevillot looks for the fish he considers Bali's best: 'Sea bream, mahi mahi, skate and snapper are excellent, but for me the greatest fun is the unexpected. Sometimes you see a fish they've caught that nobody can identify.'

Visiting the Market

Tourists can wander through the market during the day, but Chevillot's advice is simple: 'Get &there early, and then stay out of the way. Wander around the dark interior and be ready to be constantly surprised.'

Although this is very much a working fish market, the vendors actually are happy to see visitors, figuring they will eat more seafood.

When a new boat pulls up to the beach, follow the excited crowd to see what bounty has appeared.

Enjoying Jimbaran's Seafood

Jimbaran's seafood warungs draw visitors from across the south. There are three distinct groups of seafood warungs spread out along the long beach. They do fresh barbecued seafood every evening (and noon at many). The open-sided affairs are right by the beach and perfect for enjoying sea breezes and sunsets. Tables and chairs are set up on the sand almost to the water's edge.

At the best places, the fish is soaked in a garlic and lime marinade, then doused with chilli and oil while it's grilling over coconut husks. Roaming bands perform tunes from the 'I've got to be me' playlist. In the Eating section we recommend the best place for a meal in each of the three groups.

Selling fish on the beach

which have a certain raffish charm. (off Jl Pantai Jimbaran; meals 80,000-200,000Rp)

Blue Marlin   SEAFOOD $$

7 🍴   Map p62, C1

The longest row of seafood restaurants is the northern group just south of the fish market. This is where a taxi will take you if you don't specify otherwise. Most of these places are like this brick-clad establishment: restaurant-like with tables inside and out on the immaculate raked sand. Call for free transport to/from much of the south. (Jl Pantai Kedonganan; meals 80,000-200,000Rp)

Shopping

Jenggala Keramik Bali   CERAMICS

8 🔒   Map p62, C5

This modern warehouse showcases beautiful ceramic homewares that are a favourite Balinese purchase. There's a viewing area where you can watch production, and a cafe. Ceramic courses are available for adults and children. (Jl Ulu Watu II; ⏱9am-6pm)

Warung Bamboo   SEAFOOD $$

6 🍴   Map p62, B3

The middle seafood warungs are a compact group just south of Jl Pantai Jimbaran and Jl Pemelisan Agung junction. They are simple affairs, with old-fashioned thatched roofs and open sides. The beach is a little more natural, with the fishing boats up on the sand. Warung Bamboo is slightly more appealing than its neighbours, all of

Explore

Ulu Watu & Around

World-famous surf breaks proceed down the west coast of the Bukit Peninsula like a perfect set of waves. Board riders are drawn from across the world. Most visitors, however, are mere surfing poseurs and come for the idyllic little beaches at the base of the cliffs. And no visit is complete without a visit to Ulu Watu's monkey-filled temple.

The Region in a Day

☀ Get your board and get in the water. While others are sleeping off the night before you can surf legendary breaks like **Ulu Watu** (p72), with fewer crowds than later in the day. (And if you do wish you'd slept off the night before, think of the bracing qualities of the waves...)

☀ Some may just keep surfing but most visitors will thrill to the many nooks and crannies of the Bukit Peninsula. The great little beaches like **Balangan** (p69), **Bingin** (p69) and **Padang Padang** (p69) are great finds that are worth minor treks across bad roads and steep cliffside trails and stairs. Settle back on a lounger, enjoy a cold drink from a simple cafe and watch the surf action on the breaks offshore.

☾ Little places to stay – from simple surfer dives to posh boutique hotels – are where non-daytrippers vanish to after dark (nightlife is very limited). But everyone – including daytrippers – should make time for **Pura Luhur Ulu Watu** (p71) near sunset. The temple and its views are great and the **dance performance** (p75) is a must.

 Top Experiences

Hanging Out at Ulu Watu's Beaches (p68)

💗 **Best of Bali**

Surf Breaks

Ulu Watu (p72)

Balangan (p71)

Bingin (p71)

Impossibles (p71)

Beaches

Balangan Beach (p69)

Padang Padang Beach (p69)

For Kids

Pura Luhur Ulu Watu (p71)

Getting There & Around

🚗 **Taxi** Taxis from the Kuta–Seminyak area to the beaches along the Bukit Peninsula and Ulu Watu will cost 125,000Rp to 200,000Rp one way. If daytripping, be sure to arrange for a return as taxis don't hang around. Ulu Watu temple is often on tour itineraries.

Walk The various beaches are isolated from each other, so getting from one to the next requires some effort.

Top Experiences
Hanging Out at Ulu Watu's Beaches

One of Bali's hotspots is the booming west coast of the Bukit Peninsula with its string-of-pearls beaches. Often hidden at the base of cliffs, these white-sand visions of sunny pleasure are some of the best on Bali. You may have to drive along a road that barely qualifies as such and clamber down a steep path, but the reward is always worth it. Lazing away an afternoon at one of these coves is an essential part of Bali.

Bingin Beach

Don't Miss

Balangan Beach

Balangan Beach (Map p70, C1) is a real find. A long and low strand at the base of the cliffs is covered with palm trees and fronted by a ribbon of near-white sand, picturesquely dotted with white sun umbrellas. Surfer bars (some with bare-bones sleeping rooms), cafes in shacks and even slightly more permanent guesthouses precariously line the shore where buffed first-world bods soak up rays amid third-world sanitation. Balangan Beach is 6.5km off the main Ulu Watu road via Cenggiling.

Bingin Beach

An ever-evolving scene, Bingin (Map p70, C2) comprises several funky lodgings scattered across cliffs and on the strip of white sand below. A 1km rocky road turns off the paved road (look for the thicket of accommodation signs), which in turn branches off the main Ulu Watu road at the small village of Pecatu. After you pay an elderly resident for access, you access the beach from a main parking area. Follow the steep steps and trail down.

Padang Padang Beach

Small in size but not in perfection, this little cove (Map p70, B2) is near the main Ulu Watu road where a stream flows into the sea. Parking is easy and it is a short walk through a temple and down a well-paved trail. If you are feeling adventurous, a much longer stretch of white sand begins on the west side of the river. Ask locals how to get there.

☑ **Top Tips**

▸ Most of the beaches have namesake surf breaks offshore. Nonsurfers – who predominate – enjoy watching the action on the water.

▸ Low-key beach cafes and vendors can be found on every beach.

▸ Although lacking sand, the cliffs at the Ulu Watu surf break have cafes with terraces, sun loungers and killer views.

▸ If you don't have your own transport (this is prime motorbike territory), arrange with your taxi or driver for pickup at the end of the day.

✗ **Take a Break**

Rickety bamboo supports a lounging/drinking area at **Nasa Café** (Balangan Beach; meals from 30,000Rp), where the view through the tufted palm leaves is of impossibly blue water streaked with white surf. Simple food, simple rooms and simple fun rule here and at similar joints on this tiny strip.

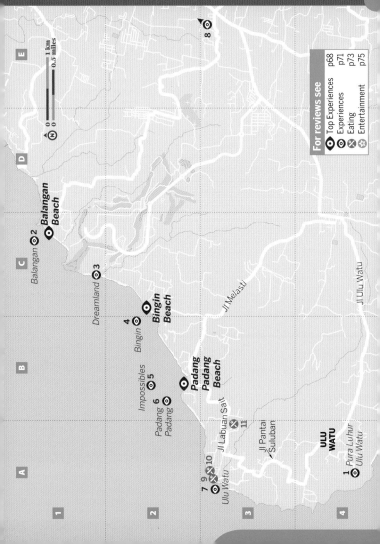

For reviews see

Top Experiences   p68
Experiences   p71
Eating   p73
Entertainment   p75

1 km
0.5 miles

E

D

C

B

A

1

2

3

4

8

Balangan
Beach

Balangan 2

Dreamland 3

Bingin
Beach

Bingin 4

Impossibles 5

Padang
Padang
Beach

Padang 6
Padang

Jl Melasti

Jl Labuan Sait

Jl Pantai
Suluban

11

7 9 10

Ulu Watu

ULU
WATU

Pura Luhur
Ulu Watu

1

Jl Ulu Watu

Jl Ulu Watu

Experiences

Pura Luhur Ulu Watu TEMPLE

1 Map p70, A4

Pura Luhur Ulu Watu is one of Bali's most important temple complexes; it's perched precariously on the south-western tip of the peninsula, atop sheer cliffs that drop straight into the pounding surf. You enter through an unusual arched gateway flanked by statues of Ganesha. Only Hindu worshippers can enter the small inner temple. But the real attraction is the location: the views out to sea seem to reach Africa (okay, Madagascar). (admission 20,000Rp, incl sarong & sash rental; ⊙8am-7pm)

Balangan SURF BREAK

2 Map p70, C1

Off the long strip of sand that is Balangan Beach, the namesake surf break is a fast left over a shallow

---

☑ Top Tip

Damn Monkeys

Pura Luhur Ulu Watu is home to scores of grey monkeys. They're greedy little rascals: when they're not energetically fornicating they snatch sunglasses, handbags, hats and anything else within reach. Of course if you want to start a riot, show them your banana...

---

reef, unsurfable at low tide and good at midtide with anything over a 4ft swell; with an 8ft swell, this can be one of the classic waves.

Dreamland SURF BREAK

3 Map p70, C1

You have to go through the sprawling, soul-destroying Pecatu Indah development to reach this break, but the waves are still here. At low 5ft swell, this solid peak offers a short, sharp right and a longer more tubular left.

Bingin SURF BREAK

4 Map p70, B2

Given the walk down to Bingin Beach from the isolated parking area, you could be forgiven if you decide to leave your board up top, but don't. Waves here are best at midtide with a 6ft swell, when short but perfect left-hand barrels are formed, and you'll do well to have somebody on shore recording your action.

Impossibles SURF BREAK

5 Map p70, B2

This outside reef break has three shifting peaks with fast left-hand tube sections that can join up if the conditions are perfect (low tide, 5ft swell), but don't stay on for too long, or you'll run out of water. It can be reached with a long paddle from either Bingin Beach or Padang Padang Beach.

Padang Padang   SURF BREAK

6 ⊙ Map p70, B2

Just 'Padang' for short, this super-shallow, left-hand reef break is offshore from the beach. If you can't surf tubes, backhand or forehand, don't go out: Padang is a tube. Many have compared it to a washing machine: it's not a spot for the faint-hearted.

Ulu Watu   SURF BREAK

7 ⊙ Map p70, A3

When the surf at Kuta Beach is 5ft to 6ft, Ulu Watu, the most famous surfing break in Bali, will be 6ft to 8ft with bigger sets. It is 1km north of Pura Luhur Ulu Watu; look for the packs of scooters equipped with surfboard racks running down either of two roads that access parking areas and the flock of cafes and surf shops that line the cliffs overlooking the breaks.

Garuda Wisnu Kencana Cultural Park   VIEWPOINT

8 ⊙ Map p70, E3

This yet-to-be-completed huge cultural park is meant to be home to a 66m-high statue of Garuda. So far the head's done – it's a biggie – and the landscaping is ace, but other signs of progress are few. It's worth stopping here on your way to Ulu Watu just for

Catching a ride, Ulu Watu

PAUL KENNEDY/LONELY PLANET IMAGES ©

the views across South Bali. If it's a clear day and you can see the volcanoes, you can't do better on the island. (📞0361-703603; admission 15,000Rp, parking 5000Rp; ⏱8am-6pm; 🚻)

Eating

Delpi Rock Lounge   CAFE $

9 🍴 Map p70, A3

The cliffs above the main Ulu Watu surf break are lined with a hodge-podge of cafes and guesthouses; some cling to rocks over the waves. At this branch of the Delpi empire, you nab a sunbed on a platform atop a rock nearly surrounded by surf. You can enter the area from the east (crowded) or from the south (a pretty walk). (Ulu Watu; meals from 50,000Rp)

Single Fin   CAFE $

10 🍴 Map p70, A3

Right near the east parking area above the Ulu Watu surf break and cliffs, this is a top spot for those who don't want to clamber down the steep concrete steps to the cafes close to the action. The views are panoramic and you can choose from a classic beach menu of sandwiches, seafood and Indo fare. The cocktail list reflects the splash of style at the bar. (Ulu Watu; meals from 50,000Rp)

Yeye's Warung   CAFE $

11 🍴 Map p70, A3

A gathering point away from the cliffs at Padang Padang, Yeye's has an easygoing ambience, cheapish beers and tasty Indonesian, Western and

---

Understand
Surfing the Bukit

With so many surf breaks – and surfers – along the west coast of the Bukit Peninsula, it's essential to know a little bit in advance. Observe where other surfers paddle out and follow them. If you are in doubt, ask someone. This can be especially true at Ulu Watu, where just getting in and out of the water through the cave at the base of the cliff can be a huge challenge.

Also understand that the breaks can get very crowded, especially on weekends and days when conditions are ideal. Here's how to fit in with the locals according to a local surfer. First, be polite! The local guys are usually cool but will stick up for each other if a tourist tries to steal a wave. If there are 50 surfers at a popular spot going for the same wave, let the locals have it and go down the beach a bit to where it's less crowded: you have a lot of choices.

Understand
Bali's History

There are few traces of Stone Age people in Bali, although it's certain that the island was populated very early in prehistoric times. By the 9th century Bali had a society based on growing rice with the help of a complex irrigation system, probably very like that employed now; the Balinese had also begun to develop their rich cultural and artistic traditions.

Hinduism followed hot on the heels of wider cultural development, and as Islam swept through neighbouring Java in the following centuries, the kings and courtiers of the embattled Hindu Majapahit kingdom began crossing the straits into Bali, making their final exodus in 1478. The priest Nirartha brought many of the complexities of the Balinese Hindu religion to the island.

Europeans Arrive

The first Europeans to set foot in Bali itself were Dutch seamen in 1597. At that time, Balinese prosperity and artistic activity, at least among the royalty, was at a peak. By the 18th century, bickering among various Balinese princes caused the island's power structure to fragment. In 1846 the Dutch landed military forces in northern Bali. Focus turned to the south, and in 1906 Dutch warships appeared at Sanur.

The Dutch forces landed despite Balinese opposition and had complete control of the island by 1908. Many thousands of Balinese – including royalty and priests – chose suicide in battle rather than occupation. Although under Dutch control and part of the Dutch East Indies, there was little development in Bali, and the common people noticed little difference between Dutch and royal rule.

Freedom

The Japanese occupied Bali in 1942 and conditions during WWII were grim. In August 1945, just days after the Japanese surrender, Soekarno, a prominent nationalist, proclaimed Indonesia's independence. Battles raged in Bali and elsewhere until the Dutch gave up and recognised Indonesia's independence in 1949. A prominent freedom fighter was Gusti Ngurah Rai, namesake of Bali's airport.

The tourism boom, which started in the early 1970s, has brought enormous changes for better and worse. However, Bali's unique culture has proved to be remarkably resilient even as visitor numbers top three million per year.

Understand
Religious Etiquette

Just because the monkeys are misbehaving at Ulu Watu doesn't mean you can. The following are basic rules for visiting temples across Bali.

▶ If visiting a temple, cover shoulders and knees. A *selandong* (traditional scarf) or sash plus a sarong is usually provided for a small donation or as part of the admission fee.

▶ Women are asked not to enter temples if they're menstruating, pregnant or have recently given birth. At these times women are thought to be *sebel* (ritually unclean).

▶ Don't put yourself higher than a priest, particularly at festivals.

vegetarian food. Many gather at night for the pizza. (Jl Labuan Sait; meals from 30,000Rp)

Entertainment

Kecak Dance TRADITIONAL DANCE

Although the performance obviously caters for tourists, the gorgeous set-ting at Pura Luhur Ulu Watu (see 7 ⭐ Map p70, A3) in a small amphitheatre in a leafy part of the grounds makes it one of the more evocative on the island. The views out to sea are as inspiring as the dance. (Pura Luhur Ulu Watu; admission 80,000Rp; ☺sunset; ⛎)

Explore

Nusa Dua
& Tanjung Benoa

Popular with holidaymakers who love large resorts, Nusa Dua seems far removed from Bali. In fact its huge beachside hotels and their hundreds of rooms could be anywhere in the world. It's a gated enclave where weeds – like uninvited locals – are marked for removal. Just to the north, slightly tatty Tanjung Benoa has a beach resort vibe without the artificial gloss.

The Region in a Day

☀ Mornings are active: start with a market visit as part of the **Bumbu Bali Cooking School** (p79). Be wet and silly at Tanjung Benoa's many water sports operators like **Benoa Marine Recreation** (p80). Straddle a banana boat and let the good times flow.

☀ Think cool for the afternoon: go for a languid stroll on the **beach promenade** (p79) or seek out the placid waters south of **Gegar Beach** (p79). Peruse beautiful Balinese art in the shady **Pasifika Museum** (p79) or lose yourself at a spa, such as the heavenly one at the **Amanusa Resort** (p79).

☾ At night all the resorts offer an array of restaurants not unlike those found at resorts the world over. Opt instead for one of the island's best: the fabulous Balinese fare at **Bumbu Bali** (p80). Afterwards you might return to the beach promenade for a moonlit stroll with the heavenly light twinkling on the calm inshore waters.

 Best of Bali

Pampering
Amanusa Spa (p79)

Eating
Bumbu Bali (p80)

Bali For Kids
Benoa Marine Recreation (p80)

Art
Pasifika Museum (p79)

Getting There & Around

🚗 **Taxi** Taxis from the airport will cost 100,000Rp to 150,000Rp. Metered taxis to/from Seminyak will cost about 90,000Rp. Note that the main road to the rest of Bali can get bogged down in traffic.

Walk A fine beach promenade runs much of the length of Nusa Dua and Tanjung Benoa. Otherwise, wide sidewalks abound in the former while the latter offers pedestrian peril along Jl Pratama.

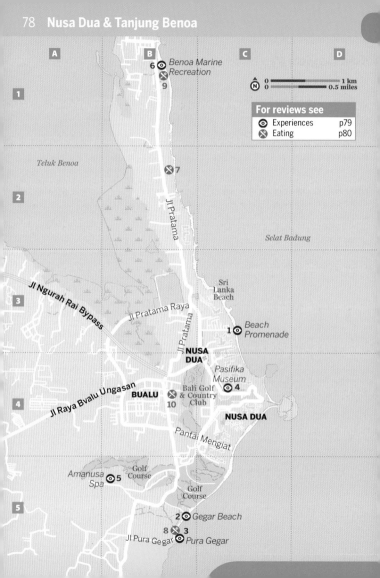

A   B   C   D

6 Benoa Marine Recreation
9

N
0 ———————— 1 km
0 ———————— 0.5 miles

For reviews see
Experiences   p79
Eating   p80

Teluk Benoa

7

Jl Pratama

Selat Badung

Jl Ngurah Rai Bypass

Sri Lanka Beach

Jl Pratama Raya

Jl Pratama

1 Beach Promenade

NUSA DUA

Pasifika Museum
4

BUALU

Jl Raya Bualu Ungasan

Bali Golf & Country Club
10

NUSA DUA

Pantai Mengiat

Amanusa Spa 5

Golf Course

Golf Course

2 Gegar Beach

8 3
Jl Pura Gegar   Pura Gegar

Experiences

Beach Promenade   WALKING

1 Map p78, C3

One of the nicest features of Nusa Dua is the 5km-long beach promenade that stretches the length of the resort and continues north along much of the beach in Tanjung Benoa. Not only is it a good stroll at any time but it also makes it easy to sample the pleasures of the other beachside resorts. The beaches along the walk are all clean; offshore reefs mean that surf sounds are almost nil.

Gegar Beach   BEACH

2 Map p78, B5

Gegar Beach has a string of tidy stands on the sand that offer drinks and snacks plus a few that rent out umbrellas, loungers and water sports gear for kayaking, windsurfing etc. A new mega-resort nearby has hemmed in the beach, but head to the south and you'll find clear, calm waters below the temple. Reefs offshore mean that the surf close in is feeble (aka kid-friendly).

Pura Gegar   TEMPLE

3 Map p78, B5

Just south of Gegar Beach is a bluff with a good cafe and a path that leads up to Pura Gegar, a compact temple shaded by gnarled old trees. Views are great and you can spy on swimmers who've come south in the shallow,

placid waters around the bluff for a little frolic.

Bumbu Bali Cooking School   COOKING SCHOOL

Heinz von Holzen runs this much-lauded cooking school at his restaurant (see **8** Map p78, B5) that strives to get to the roots of Balinese cooking. It starts with a 6am visit to Jimbaran's fish and morning markets, continues in the large kitchen and finishes with lunch. (☏0361-774502; www.balifoods.com; Jl Pratama, Tanjung Benoa; course US$90; ☼6am-3pm)

Pasifika Museum   MUSEUM

4 Map p78, C4

When groups from the nearby resorts aren't around, you'll probably have this large museum to yourself. Several centuries of art from cultures around the Pacific Ocean are displayed (the tikis are cool). The influential wave of European artists who thrived in Bali in the early 20th century is well represented. Look for works by Arie Smit, Adrien Jean Le Mayeur de Merpes and Theo Meier. (☏0361-774559; Bali Collection, Block P, Nusa Dua; admission 60,000Rp; ☼10am-6pm)

Amanusa Spa   SPA

5 Map p78, B5

The vaunted Amanusa Resort sets itself apart from Nusa's huge hotels with personal service, especially at its spa. Balinese and Swedish are among the massage techniques on offer, spa

The delights of Bumbu Bali

products are organic and a reiki master is ready to 'redress energy imbalances'. (☎0361-772333; www.amanresorts.com; Nusa Dua; massage from US$60)

Local Life
Benoa's Places of Worship

The village of **Benoa** (Map p78, B1) is a fascinating little fishing settlement that makes for a good stroll. Amble the narrow lanes of the peninsula's tip for a multicultural feast. Within 100m of each other are a brightly coloured **Chinese Buddhist temple**, a domed **mosque** and a **Hindu temple** with a nicely carved triple entrance. Enjoy views of the busy channel to the port.

Benoa Marine Recreation

WATER SPORTS

6 ◉ Map p78, B1

One of many water sport centres along the beach in Tanjung Benoa, BMR has a slightly more slick operation than the others, but all rumble in the mornings as the buses pull in with day-tripping groups. (☎0361-77 1757; Jl Pratama, Tanjung Benoa)

Eating
Bumbu Bali

BALINESE $$$

7 ✖ Map p78, B2

Long-time resident and cookbook author Heinz von Holzen, his wife Puji and an enthusiastic staff serve exquisitely flavoured dishes at this superb restaurant. Many diners opt for one of several set menus (from 225,000Rp). The *rijstaffel* shows the range of cooking in the kitchen from satays served on their own little coconut husk grill to the tender *be celeng base manis* (pork in sweet soy sauce) with a dozen more courses in between. (☏0361-774502; Jl Pratama, Tanjung Benoa; ◷noon-9pm)

Nusa Dua Beach Grill

INTERNATIONAL $

8 🍴 Map p78, B5

A hidden gem, this warm-hued cafe is just south of Gegar Beach on foot, but a circuitous 1.5km by car via the temple. The drinks menu is long, the seafood fresh and the atmosphere heavy with assignations. Lounge your afternoon away in the laid-back bar. (Jl Pura Gegar; meals 50,000-150,000Rp)

Tao

ASIAN $$

9 🍴 Map p78, B1

On its own swath of pure-white sand, Tao is one of the few options for a leisurely lunch right by the beach in Tanjung Benoa. Although it is part of the Ramada Resort, the hotel is across the street and Tao avoids the 'sign-for-it' vibe. A large curling pool wends

between the tables. The food is an eclectic mix of Asian (but a club sandwich awaits philistines). (www.taobali.com; Jl Pratama 96, Tanjung Benoa; ♿)

Warung Dobiel

BALINESE $

10 🍴 Map p78, B4

A bit of authentic joy amid the bland streets of Nusa, this warung celebrates pork. And what pork it is! The succulent pork satay is marinated for hours before it's grilled. The pork soup really is the perfect taste-bud awakener, while the jackfruit is redolent with spices. Diners perch on stools and share tables. (Jl Sri Kandi, Nusa Dua; ◷10am-3pm; meals from 25,000Rp)

Explore

Sanur

The first Western artists to settle in Bali did so around Sanur over 100 years ago. It's easy to see why: there's a long family-friendly beach protected by reefs, plenty of shady palm trees overhead and cool breezes off the ocean. Sanur will never be known as a party town, but visitors looking for serenity will be suitably chilled out.

The Region in a Day

☀ Take advantage of the eastern light to hit **Sanur Beach** (p85) in the morning. Watch people fishing in traditional ways and try some water fun from **Surya Water Sports** (p86). Or get serious and get your scuba certification at **Crystal Divers** (p85).

☼ Enjoy a leisurely lunch with views over the water to Nusa Lembongan and Nusa Penida. **Bonsai Cafe** (p86) and **Stiff Chili** (p88) are fine options. Once past midday, the shadows of the palm trees lengthen on the beach, so now is a good time for some spa action at **Jamu Traditional Spa** (p86) or **Glo Day Spa** (p86). Or just hit the shops. Jl Tamblingan has many choices including **A-Krea** (p89) for Bali-designed goods and **Ganesha Bookshop** (p89) for a perfect poolside read.

☾ For dinner, Jl Tamblingan again offers many choices. Try something Italian at **Massimo** (p87) or go with Asian flair at **Three Monkeys Cafe** (p86). At the latter you can hear live jazz some nights. Finish off your evening with a stroll on the **Beachfront Walk** (p85), which ideally will offer moonlit views over the water.

 Best of Bali

Diving & Snorkelling
Crystal Divers (p85)

Surya Water Sports (p86)

Beaches
Sanur Beach (p85)

Pampering
Jamu Traditional Spa (p86)

Bali for Kids
Sanur Beach (p85)

Surya Water Sports (p86)

Bali Kite Festival (p89)

Art
Museum Le Mayeur (p85)

Getting There & Around

🚗 **Taxi** Taxis from the airport will cost about 110,000Rp. A cab to/from Seminyak will cost about 70,000Rp and take from 20 minutes to an hour depending on traffic.

Walk You can easily walk the length of Sanur on the lovely beachfront walk. The main spine, Jl Tamblingan, is easily walkable.

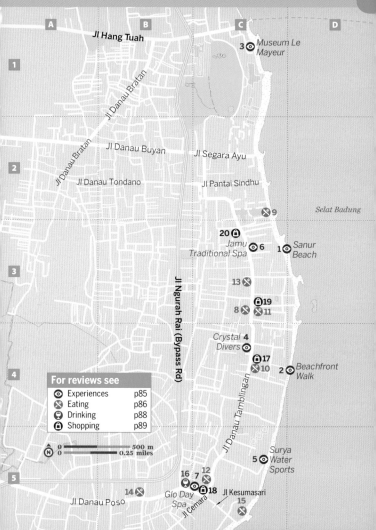

A
B
C
D

Jl Hang Tuah

1

3 Museum Le Mayeur

Jl Danau Bratan

Jl Danau Bratan

Jl Danau Buyan

Jl Segara Ayu

2

Jl Danau Tondano

Jl Pantai Sindhu

Selat Badung

9

20

Jamu 6
Traditional Spa

1 Sanur Beach

3

13

19

Jl Ngurah Rai (Bypass Rd)

8 11

Crystal 4
Divers

17
10 2 Beachfront Walk

4

Jl Danau Tamblingan

For reviews see

◉	Experiences	p85
⊗	Eating	p86
⊖	Drinking	p88
🔒	Shopping	p89

N
0   500 m
0   0.25 miles

Surya
Water
5 Sports

5

16 7 12

14

Jl Danau Poso

Glo Day 18
Spa

Jl Kesumasari

Jl Cemara

15

Experiences

Sanur Beach BEACH

1 Map p84, C3

Sanur's beach curves in a southwesterly direction and stretches for over 5km. It is mostly clean and overall quite serene – much like the town itself. Offshore reefs mean that the surf is reduced to tiny waves lapping the shore. With a couple of unfortunate exceptions, the resorts along the sand are low-key, leaving the beach uncrowded.

Beachfront Walk PROMENADE

2 Map p84, C4

Sanur's beachfront walk was the first in Bali and has been delighting locals and visitors alike from day one. Over 4km long, it curves past resorts, beachfront cafes, wooden fishing boats under repair and quite a few elegant old villas built decades ago by the wealthy expats who fell under Bali's spell. While you stroll, look out across the water to Nusa Penida.

Museum Le Mayeur MUSEUM

3 Map p84, C1

Exquisite paintings by Adrien Jean Le Mayeur de Merpes (1880–1958) are on display in his old compound on the beach at the north end of Sanur's seafront. Paintings from his early period in Bali are romantic depictions of daily life and beautiful Balinese women including his elegant wife, Ni

Polok. The works from the 1950s show the vibrant colours that later became popular with young Balinese artists. (☎0361-286201; adult/child 2000/1000Rp; ⏱7.30am-3.30pm)

Crystal Divers DIVING

4 Map p84, C4

This slick diving operation has its own hotel and a large diving pool right outside the office. Recommended for beginners, the shop offers a long list of courses, including PADI open-water for US$450. (☎0361-286737; www.crystal-divers.com; Jl Tamblingan 168; intro dives from US$60)

CLAUDE THIBAULT/ALAMY ©

Flying high on Sanur Beach

☑️ Top Tip

Bali's Oldest Artefact?

A **Stone Pillar** (Map p84, B5), down a narrow lane to the left as you face Pura Belangjong, is Bali's oldest dated artefact and has ancient inscriptions recounting military victories of more than a thousand years ago. These inscriptions are in Sanskrit and are evidence of Hindu influence 300 years before the arrival of the Majapahit court. This is a good excuse for a non-beach walk up here followed by a meal at Sari Bundo.

Surya Water Sports   WATER SPORTS

5 🎯 Map p84, C5

One of several water sports operations along the beach, Surya is the largest. You can go parasailing (US$20 per ride), snorkelling by boat (US$35, two hours), windsurfing (US$30, one hour) or rent a kayak and paddle the smooth waters (US$5 per hour). (📞0361-287956; Jl Duyung 10; ⏰9am-5pm; 🚹)

Jamu Traditional Spa   SPA

6 🎯 Map p84, C3

The beautifully carved teak and stone entry sets the mood at this gracious spa, which offers a range of treatments including a popular earth-and-flower body mask and a kemiri nut scrub. Can't you just feel the 'ahhhhh-hhh'? (📞0361-286595; www.jamutraditional spa.com; Jl Tamblingan 41; massage from 550,000Rp)

Glo Day Spa   SPA

7 🎯 Map p84, C5

An insider pick by the many local Sanur expats, Glo eschews a fancy setting for a clean-lined storefront. Services and treatments span the gamut, from skin and nail care to massages and spa therapies. (📞0361-282826; www.glo-day-spa.com; Gopa Town Centre, Jl Danau Poso 57; sessions from 150,000Rp; ⏰8am-6pm)

Eating

Three Monkeys Cafe   CAFE $$

8 🍴 Map p84, C3

This branch of the splendid Ubud original is no mere knock-off: spread over two floors, there's cool jazz playing in the background and live performances some nights. Set well back from the road, you can enjoy Sanur's best coffee drinks on sofas or chairs. The menu mixes healthy Western fare with pan-Asian creations. (Jl Tamblingan; meals 60,000-150,000Rp; 📶)

Bonsai Cafe   CAFE $

9 🍴 Map p84, C2

Although the menu is all beachside standards (and good ones), the real reason to seek this place out is for the proof that the name is not notional: there are hundreds of bonsai trees in sizes from tiny to small. (Jl Tamblingan 27; meals 40,000-90,000Rp; 📶)

Cafe Batu Jimbar CAFE, BAKERY **$$**

10 🍴 Map p84, C4

Although pricey, this attractive cafe has a shady wooden patio fronting an airy dining room. Succumb to the best banana smoothie in Bali, then let the luscious baked goods work their magic. A gourmet grocery adjoins. (📞0361-287374; Jl Tamblingan 152; 👶)

Café Smorgås CAFE **$$**

11 🍴 Map p84, C3

Set back from traffic, this sprightly place has nice wicker chairs outside and cool air-con inside. The menu

has a healthy bent: try a detox drink (the opposite of fun for many...) and then live it up with quiche or carrot cake. (📞0361-289361; Jl Tamblingan; meals 50,000-150,000Rp; 🍴)

Massimo ITALIAN **$$**

12 🍴 Map p84, C5

The interior is like an open-air Milan cafe, the outside like a Balinese garden – a combo that goes together like spaghetti and meatballs. Pasta, pizza and more are prepared with authentic Italian flair. No time for a meal? Nab some gelati from the counter up front. (📞0361-288942; Jl Tamblingan 206; meals 80,000-200,000Rp)

Understand
Sanur's Rulers & Artists

Sanur was one of the places favoured by Westerners during their pre-WWII discovery of Bali. Artists Miguel Covarrubias, Adrien Jean Le Mayeur de Merpes and Walter Spies, anthropologist Jane Belo and choreographer Katharane Mershon all spent time here. The first tourist bungalows appeared in Sanur in the 1940s and '50s, and retiring expats followed.

During this period Sanur was ruled by insightful priests and scholars, who recognised both the opportunities and the threats presented by expanding tourism. Horrified at the high-rise Grand Bali Beach Hotel, they imposed the famous rule that no building could be higher than a coconut palm. They also established village cooperatives that owned land and ran tourist businesses, ensuring that economic benefits remained in the community.

The priestly influence remains strong, and Sanur is one of the few communities still ruled by members of the Brahmana caste. It is known as a home of sorcerers and healers, and a centre for both black and white magic. The black-and-white chequered cloth known as *kain poleng,* which symbolises the balance of good and evil, is emblematic of Sanur.

Porch Cafe

CAFE $

13 Map p84, C3

Fronting Flashbacks, a charmer of a small hotel, this cafe is housed in a traditional wooden building replete with the namesake porch. Snuggle up to a table out front or shut it all out in the air-con inside. The menu is a tasty mix of comfort food like burgers and freshly baked goods. Popular for breakfast; there's a long list of fresh juices. (📞0361-281682; Jl Tamblingan; meals from 40,000Rp; 🛜)

Sari Bundo

INDONESIAN $

14 Map p84, B5

This spotless Padang-style shopfront is one of several at the south end of Sanur. Choose from an array of fresh and very spicy food. The curry chicken is a fiery treat that will have your tongue alternately loving and hating you. (📞0361-281389; Jl Danau Poso; ⏱24hr)

Local Life
Sanur's Expat Bars

Seminyak may get all the posers, but Sanur gets the ones with healthy retirement accounts. Two classic expat hangouts are the **Cat & Fiddle** (Map p84, B5; 📞0361-282218; Jl Cemara 36) and **Kalimantan** (Map p84, C2; 📞0361-289291; Jl Pantai Sindhu 11), aka Borneo Bob's.

Coconut indulgence, Sanur

Stiff Chili

INTERNATIONAL $$

15  Map p84, C5

Apart from the evocative name, this beachside cafe has fine views through its near lack of walls. Pizza and pasta head the surprisingly ambitious menu. (Jl Kesumasari; meals 50,000-140,000Rp)

Drinking

Cafe Billiard

BAR

16  Map p84, B5

Drawing a well-lubricated expat crowd, this open-air place keeps 'em happy with billiards and cheap Heineken. Many of the regulars feel more comfortable in the commodious wicker chairs than they do at home. (Jl Danau Poso; ☉noon-1am)

Shopping

Gudang Keramik
CERAMICS

17 🔒 Map p84, C4

This is a real find. It's an outlet store for the highly regarded Jenggala Keramik Bali in Jimbaran. Prices are amazing, and what are called 'seconds' here would be firsts everywhere else. On Saturdays there is an organic farmers market in the parking lot. (Jl Tamblingan)

Brothers and Sisters
CLOTHES

18 🔒 Map p84, C5

Cute threads for cute kids. The designs are suitably light and airy for tropical holidays. What better way to strut the promenade than in cool new duds? Designed and made on Bali. (Gopa Town Centre; Jl Danau Poso 57)

A-Krea
CLOTHES

19 🔒 Map p84, C3

A range of items designed and made on Bali are available in this attractive store that takes the colours of the island and gives them a minimalist flair. Clothes, accessories, housewares and more are all handmade. (Jl Tamblingan 51)

Ganesha Bookshop
BOOKS

20 🔒 Map p84, C3

Bali's best bookshop for serious readers has a new shop in the heart of Sanur. Besides excellent choices in new and used fiction, Ganesha has superb selections on local culture and history. There's also a special reading area for kids. (Jl Tamblingan 42)

Local Life
Sanur's Kites

You hear them overhead: huge kites 10m or more in length, with tails stretching another 100m and sporting noise-makers producing eerie humming and buzzing noises. Although these enormous fliers have spiritual roots for the Balinese, for most sending kites aloft is sport.

Each July hundreds of Balinese and international teams descend – as it were – on open spaces north of Sanur for the **Bali Kite Festival**. They compete for an array of honours in such categories as original design and flight endurance. The action is centred around **Padang Galak Beach**, about 2km up the coast from Sanur. Peak time for catching the high-flying art over Sanur is May to September.

Top Experiences
Nusa Lembongan

Getting There

🚤 **Boat** Public boats from Sanur at 8am cost 60,000Rp one way and take one to 1½ hours. Fast tourist boats run by Scoot (www.scootcruise .com) cost US$50 return and include hotel pick-ups.

Alluringly seen from Sanur and east Bali, Nusa Lembongan is one of three islands that together comprise the Nusa Penida archipelago. It's the Bali many imagine but never find: rooms right on the beach, cheap beers with incredible sunsets, days spent surfing and diving, and nights spent riffling through a favourite book or hanging with new friends. You can savour this bliss in a day or two away from the bright lights of south Bali.

Views of sleepy Jungutbatu Beach

Don't Miss

Jungutbatu Beach

Jungutbatu beach, a lovely arc of white sand with clear blue water, has superb views across to Gunung Agung in Bali. The village itself is pleasant, with quiet lanes, no cars and a couple of temples.

Mushroom Bay

Gorgeous little Mushroom Bay, unofficially named for the mushroom corals offshore, has a perfect crescent of white-sand beach. The most pleasant way to get here from Jungutbatu is to walk along the trail that starts from the southern end of the main beach and follows the coastline for 1km or so past a couple of little beaches.

Diving & Snorkelling

There are great diving possibilities around the islands, from shallow and sheltered reefs to very demanding drift dives. Notable sites include **Blue Corner** and **Jackfish Point** off Nusa Lembongan. Good snorkelling can be had just off the Mushroom Bay and Bounty **pontoons** off Jungutbatu Beach, as well as in areas off the north coast of the island.

World Diving

World Diving (☎081-2390 0686; www.world-diving .com), based at Pondok Baruna on Jungutbatu Beach, is well regarded. It offers various courses; two-tank dives are from US$80, snorkelling trips are US$25.

Surfing

Surfing here is best in the dry season (April to September), when the winds come from the southeast. It's not for beginners. There are three main breaks on the reef, all aptly named. From north to south are **Shipwreck**, **Lacerations** and **Playground**.

☑ Top Tips

▸ There are lots of simple guesthouses and a few small upmarket hotels.

▸ You can charter a boat from 150,000Rp per hour for snorkelling and for getting out to some surf breaks.

▸ You can easily walk to most places; bicycles cost 30,000Rp per day.

▸ There's no ATM.

▸ A walk around much of the island is an all-day adventure.

✖ Take a Break

There are numerous beach cafes with all the usual standards plus fabulous views. For a cut above, **Indiana Kenanga** (www. indiana-kenanga-villas.com; Jungutbatu; meals US$10 to US$30; 🛜) looks plucked from a glossy magazine and has an all-day menu of seafood, sandwiches and various surprises cooked up by a French chef.

Explore

Denpasar

Bali's capital, home to most of the island's people and covering much of south Bali, shouldn't be overlooked by visitors. Chaotic and confusing streets mix with wide parks and boulevards that have a certain grandeur. The island's main museums and largest markets are here as well as a range of excellent restaurants aimed at the demanding tastes of locals.

The Region in a Day

☀ Visit the markets, **Pasar Badung** (p97) and **Pasar Kumbasari** (p97), in the morning when selection is greatest. The fruits and vegetables still look fresh and the flowers used for offerings are at their colourful best.

☀ Lunch at any of many local eateries in Renon, such as **Cak Asm** (p95) and **Ayam Goreng Kalasan** (p95), which have excellent local dishes cooked to the standards demanded by the choosy Balinese. After, absorb Bali's history and culture at the comprehensive **Museum Bali** (p95), the important temple **Pura Jagatnatha** (p95) and the surprisingly entertaining **Bajra Sandhi Monument** (p95).

☾ For visitors, Denpasar is an easy daytrip from across south Bali and Ubud. However, it offers few reasons to linger after late afternoon.

💙 Best of Bali

Shopping
Pasar Badung (p97)

Anis (p97)

Art
Museum Bali (p95)

Getting There & Around

🚕 **Taxi** Taxis from Sanur cost about 30,000Rp, from Seminyak about 50,000Rp. Expect heavy traffic.

Walk You can easily walk between the main markets and Museum Bali. Most restaurants are located in Renon, a long walk from the markets or a 10,000Rp taxi ride.

Jl Drupadi

Jl Hayam Wuruk

KEDATON

Jl Badak Agung

Jl Cok Agung Tresna

Jl Dr Kusuma Atmaja

Bajra Sandhi
Monument **3**

Jl Panjaitan

Jl Tjut Nyak Dien

Letda Tantular

Jl Raya Puputan

Jl Surapati

Jl Jayagiri

Jl Ki Hajar Dewantara

RENON

Pura
Jagatnatha
2

Museum
Bali **1**

Jl Kapten Agung

Jl Udayana

Jl Sudirman

Jl Gajah Mada

Jl Sumatra

Jl Diponegoro

Jl Hasanudin

Jl Kartini

7

6
8

Jl Thamrin

Sungai Badung

Jl Nusakambangan

Jl Teuku Umar

For reviews see

Experiences p95
Eating   p95
Shopping   p97

400 m
0.2 miles

The Region in a Day

☀ Visit the markets, **Pasar Badung** (p97) and **Pasar Kumbasari** (p97), in the morning when selection is greatest. The fruits and vegetables still look fresh and the flowers used for offerings are at their colourful best.

☀ Lunch at any of many local eateries in Renon, such as **Cak Asm** (p95) and **Ayam Goreng Kalasan** (p95), which have excellent local dishes cooked to the standards demanded by the choosy Balinese. After, absorb Bali's history and culture at the comprehensive **Museum Bali** (p95), the important temple **Pura Jagatnatha** (p95) and the surprisingly entertaining **Bajra Sandhi Monument** (p95).

☾ For visitors, Denpasar is an easy daytrip from across south Bali and Ubud. However, it offers few reasons to linger after late afternoon.

💜 Best of Bali

Shopping
Pasar Badung (p97)

Anis (p97)

Art
Museum Bali (p95)

Getting There & Around

🚗 **Taxi** Taxis from Sanur cost about 30,000Rp, from Seminyak about 50,000Rp. Expect heavy traffic.

Walk You can easily walk between the main markets and Museum Bali. Most restaurants are located in Renon, a long walk from the markets or a 10,000Rp taxi ride.

JI Drupadi

JI Cok Agung Tresna

JI Dr Kusumah Atmaja

3

Bajra Sandhi
Monument

JI Hayam Wuruk

KEDATON

JI Badak Agung

JI Panjaitan

JI Tjut Nyak Dien

JI Raya Puputan

5

JI Jayagiri

Letda Tantular

JI Surapati

JI Ki Hajar Dewantara

RENON

Pura
Jagatnatha
2

1

JI Kapten Agung

Museum
Bali

JI Udayana

JI Sudirman

JI Gajah Mada

JI Sumatra

JI Diponegoro

JI Kartini

7

Sungai Badung

JI Teuku Umar

6
8

JI Hasanudin

JI Nusakhambangan

JI Thamrin

For reviews see

Experiences   p95
Eating   p95
Shopping   p97

400 m
0.2 miles

Experiences

Museum Bali
MUSEUM

1 ⊙ Map p94, B1

This museum comprises several buildings and pavilions, including examples of the architecture of both the *puri* (palace) and *pura* (temple), with features such as a *candi bentar* (split gateway) and a *kulkul* (warning drum) tower. Among the old artefacts, look for the fine wood-and-cane carrying cases for transporting fighting cocks, and tiny carrying cases for fighting crickets. It's all a little dusty and never crowded, but it's an invaluable primer in Bali 101. (☎0361-222680; adult/child 10,000/5000Rp; ⊙8am-12.30pm Fri, 8am-3pm Sat-Thu)

Pura Jagatnatha
TEMPLE

2 ⊙ Map p94, B1

Next to the museum, the state temple is dedicated to the supreme god, Sanghyang Widi. Pause at the *padmasana* (shrine) made of white coral. It consists of an empty throne (symbolic of heaven) on top of the cosmic turtle and two *naga* (mythological serpents), which symbolise the foundation of the world. (JI Surapati)

Bajra Sandhi Monument
MONUMENT

3 ⊙ Map p94, E4

Inside this vaguely Borobudur-like structure, which dominates a large park in Renon, are dioramas tracing Bali's history. Taking the name as a cue (it means 'Monument to the Struggle of the People of Bali'), you'll understand the jingoistic soap-opera quality of the dolls and their mayhem. (☎0361-264517; JI Raya Puputan; adult/child 10,000/5000Rp; ⊙8.30am-5pm)

Eating

Cak Asm
BALINESE $

4 ✗ Map p94, D4

Join the government workers and students from the nearby university for superb dishes cooked to order in the bustling kitchen. Order the *cumi cumi* (calamari) with *telor asin* sauce (a heavenly mixture of eggs and garlic). The resulting buttery, crispy goodness could well be the best dish you have while you're in Bali. Fruity ice drinks are a cooling treat. (JI Tukad Gangga; meals from 25,000Rp)

Ayam Goreng Kalasan
INDONESIAN $

5 ✗ Map p94, D3

The name here says it all: fried chicken *(ayam goreng)* named for a Javanese temple (Kalasan) in a region renowned for its fiery, crispy chicken. The version here falls off the bone on the way to the table; the meat is redolent with lemongrass from a long marinade prior to the plunge into boiling oil. There are several other excellent little warungs in this strip. (JI Cok Agung Tresna 6; meals from 25,000Rp)

Understand
Bali's Dance & Music

Bali's renowned dance, which is accompanied by its unique and lyrical gamelan music, is easily enjoyed, even on a short visit. For many it is a highlight of their trip and is what sets Bali apart from other destinations.

If you visit in June and July, be sure to check out the **Bali Arts Festival** (www.baliartsfestival.com), a huge celebration of Balinese dance and music that takes place at venues in Denpasar.

Dance

Balinese love a blend of seriousness and slapstick, and this shows in their dances. Some have a decidedly comic element, with clowns who convey the story and also act as a counterpoint to the staid, noble characters. Balinese dance is precise, jerky, shifting and jumpy, remarkably like Balinese music. Every movement of wrist, hand and fingers is charged with meaning, while facial expressions are carefully choreographed to convey the character of the dance.

Probably the best known of the dances is the Kecak, which tells a tale from the *Ramayana,* one of the great Hindu holy books. Throughout performances the dancing and chanting are superbly synchronised with an eerily exciting coordination. Add in actors posing as an army of monkeys and you have an unbeatable spectacle.

Another popular dance for tourists shows a battle between good (the Barong) and bad (the Rangda). The Barong is a strange but good, mischievous and fun-loving shaggy dog-lion. The widow-witch Rangda is bad through and through.

The most graceful of Balinese dances, Legong, is performed by young girls. It is so important in Balinese culture that in old age a classic dancer will be remembered as a 'great *legong*'.

You'll find exceptional dance performances in and around Ubud. Some south Bali hotels offer abbreviated performances with just a few musicians and a couple of dancers.

Music

Balinese music is based around an ensemble known as a gamelan, also called a *gong*. A full orchestra has up to 25 shiny bronze instruments. Although it sounds strange at first with its noisy, jangly percussion, it's exciting, enjoyable, melodic and at times haunting. Gamelan is a part of most dance performances.

Local temple fun, Denpasar

Shopping

Pasar Badung
MARKET

6 🅰 Map p94, A1

Bali's largest market is busy in the morning and evening; it's a great place to browse and bargain. You'll find produce and food from all over the island, as well as easy-to-assemble temple offerings that are popular with working women. (Jl Gajah Mada)

Anis
TEXTILES

7 🅰 Map p94, A1

Jammed into a string of fabric stores just east of Pasar Badung, this narrow shop stands out for its huge selection of genuine Balinese batik. The colours and patterns are bewildering, while the clearly marked reasonable prices are not. (Jl Sulawesi 27)

Pasar Kumbasari
MARKET

8 🅰 Map p94, A1

Handicrafts, a plethora of vibrant fabrics and costumes decorated with gold are just some of the goods at this huge market across the river from Pasar Badung. Plunge into the canyons of colour. (Jl Gajah Mada)

Explore

Ubud

When you think about what really sets Bali apart from other beachy destinations, it is the culture, the rice fields and the inherent charm of the people – qualities that Ubud has in spades. Bali's rich artistic and dance traditions are here to enjoy. And there's plenty of sybaritic spas and splendid restaurants to keep things from getting too high-minded.

The Region
in a Day

☀ Get up with the sun and walk through Ubud's **rice fields** (p100). Afterwards try to think up new words for 'green' and 'beautiful' as you enjoy a coffee at one Ubud's many great cafes such as **Tutmak Cafe** (p113) or **Coffee & Silver** (p112). Now might be a good time for some shopping at the boutiques on Jl Dewi Sita.

☼ Have a healthy lunch at **Bali Buddha** (p111), or go completely local at **Warung Ibu Oka** (p112). Now enjoy some pampering. Consider yoga at **Yoga Barn** (p108), a range of spa therapies at **Taksu** (p108) or a luxurious massage at **Bali Botanica Day Spa** (p108).

☾ No night is complete without a taste of Ubud's famed culture. Choose your **dance performance** (p115) and enjoy traditions that are the very soul of the Balinese. After, savour dinner at **Mozaic** (p110), **Bridges** (p110), **Warung Pulau Kelapa** (p110) or another fine spot. Ubud goes to bed early: after a glimpse of the moonlight on the rice fields, enjoy a great night's sleep in the cool mountain air; or extend your evening with some Western tunes at the **Jazz Café** (p113).

For a local's day in Ubud, see p102.

 Top Experiences
Touring Ubud's Rice Fields (p100)

Local Life
A Perfect Ubud Day (p102)

Best of Bali

Nightlife
Jazz Café (p113)

Pampering
Bali Botanica Day Spa (p108)
Yoga Barn (p108)
Taksu (p108)
Ubud Sari Health Resort (p102)

Eating
Mozaic (p110)
Bridges (p110)

Getting There & Around

🚗 **Car** A car and driver to/from Ubud and south Bali will cost about US$25. A metered taxi will be about 150,000Rp.

Walk Ubud is all about walking, but you might not want to make the long jaunt from, say, Padangtegal and Sanggingan. Ubiquitous local guys offer 'transport' for about 20,000Rp to 40,000Rp depending on distance.

Top Experiences
Touring Ubud's Rice Fields

There's nothing like a walk through the verdant rice fields of Ubud to make all right with the world. These unbelievably green and ancient terraces spill down lush hillsides to rushing rivers below. As you wander along, you can hear the symphony of frogs, bugs and the constant gurgle of water coursing through channels. Most fields produce three crops a year, and even on a short walk you'll see tender shoots, vibrant seas of green and the grain-heavy heads of mature plants.

The peaceful rice fields of Ubud

Don't Miss

Walk It Yourself

From the Ibah Luxury Villas driveway in Campuan, take the path to the left, where a walkway crosses the river to the small and serene Pura Gunung Lebah. Follow the concrete path north onto the ridge between the two rivers where you can see the rice fields above Ubud folding over the hills in all directions.

Bali Bird Walks

For the keen birdwatcher, this popular **tour** (☎0361-975009; www.balibirdwalk.com; tour US$37; ⏱9am-12.30pm Tue, Fri, Sat & Sun) started by Victor Mason draws flocks. A gentle morning's walk will give you the opportunity to see maybe 30 of the 100 or so local species. The tours leave from the former Beggar's Bush Bar on Jl Raya Campuan.

Herb Walks

Three-hour **walks** (☎0361-975051; www.baliherbalwalk .com; walks US$18; ⏱8.30am Mon-Thu) through lush Bali landscape; medicinal and cooking herbs and plants are identified and explained in their natural environment. Includes herbal drinks.

Banyan Tree Cycling

Day-long **tours** (☎0361-805 1620, 0813-3879 8516; www.banyantree.wikispaces.com; tours from 450,000Rp) of remote villages in the hills above Ubud. It's locally owned, and the tours emphasise interaction with villagers. These are very popular and have inspired a bevy of competitors.

Bali Nature & Medicine Walk

Lifelong Ubud resident and herbalist leads customisable **walks** (☎0818-0539 9228; sangtubud@yahoo.com; price varies depending on walk) through the countryside explaining how the Balinese interact with nature.

☑ Top Tips

▶ Channel your inner duck as you explore rice fields; if a path peters out, you can always go back.

▶ Bring water, a good hat, decent shoes and wet-weather gear for the afternoon showers.

▶ Try to start walks at daybreak, before it gets too hot.

▶ Some entrepreneurial rice farmers have erected little toll gates across their fields. You can detour around them or pay a fee (never, ever accede to more than 10,000Rp).

✕ Take a Break

A healthful walk through Ubud's beautiful rice fields calls for a healthy snack. Bali Buddha (p111) has a small organic market on its ground floor where you can choose from a range of tasty treats to stash in your knapsack (snacks from 10,000Rp). The blueberry muffins are especially good.

Local Life
A Perfect Ubud Day

Spas, shopping, cafes, markets, temples, dance and more can fill your Ubud days. Here's an ideal stroll that combines a little of all, and will work whether you are staying for a few days or are a daytripper. This walk takes you through the heart of the town and you'll find plenty of discoveries along the way.

....

1 Cleanse Yourself Inside & Out

There are so many places in Ubud for health and spa treatments that you almost need therapy to sort through them. But an excellent place to start is **Ubud Sari Health Resort** (📞0361-974393; Jl Kajeng; 1hr massage from US$40; ⏰8am-8pm), where function trumps form. The setting is pastoral and includes all manner of herbs and healing plants.

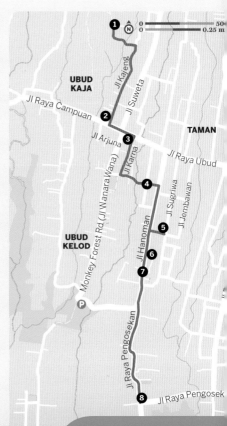

➋ Ubud's Water Temple

An oasis in the heart of Ubud, **Pura Taman Saraswati** (Jl Raya Ubud) is one of the town's most picturesque spots. Waters from the temple at the rear feed a pond overflowing with iconic lotus blossoms. There's usually a few wannabe artists trying to capture the moment. No matter how frenetic the traffic is outside, here you'll feel nothing but calm.

➌ Ubud's Hidden Produce Market

Hidden within the overcrowded and euphemistically named art market is this real, working **Produce Market** (Jl Raya Ubud; ⏰6am-1pm). Get here early enough and you'll find Ubud's top chefs bargaining for their day's ingredients. Browse Bali's fab range of fresh foodstuffs and see how many types of fruit you *can't* identify.

➍ Dewi Sita Creations

The relatively short, curving and hilly Jl Dewi Sita is lined with some of Ubud's most creative shops. Everything from handmade paper to jewellery to luscious beauty products can be found at its little boutiques.

➎ Lunch at Warung Soba

By now you're ready for some nourishment. Nowhere embodies the Ubud vibe better than **Warung Soba** (Jl Sugriwa 36; meals 30,000-60,000Rp; 🖊📶). Open-air and oh-so-groovy, this popular corner place has a daily menu of healthy and vegetarian fare. Most dishes are displayed enticingly, making choosing tough.

➏ Yoga Store

It can seem like every other person in Ubud is either a yoga student or a yoga teacher. Even if you're not yet either, you can get the right look at **Ubud Yoga Boutique** (Jl Hanoman), which is part of the ubiquitous Yoga Barn empire. Clothes, mats and all manner of accessories are on offer.

➐ Shopping Jl Hanoman

Ubud has myriad art shops, clothing boutiques and galleries. Some of the most interesting are found along Jl Hanoman. Take your time wandering this long, slanting street and see what discoveries you make; many shops are owned by the designers of the goods within. Stop in one of the many little cafes for a break.

➑ Dance Performance

Ubud has cultural performances virtually every night, and even if you are just visiting for a day, it's well worth staying for an evening performance before heading back to your hotel or villa in the south. One of the best venues is the **ARMA Open Stage** (📞0361-976659; Jl Raya Pengosekan) as it attracts some of the best troupes.

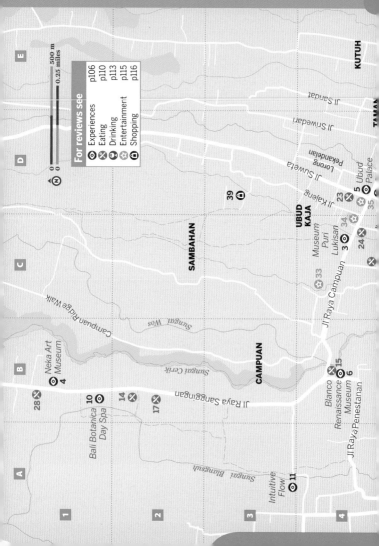

For reviews see

◎ Experiences   p106
⊗ Eating   p110
🍷 Drinking   p113
✪ Entertainment   p115
🛍 Shopping   p116

500 m
0.25 miles

KUTUH

TAMAN

Jl Sandat

Jl Sriwedari

Lorong Pekandelan

Jl Suweta

Ubud Palace

5 ◎
35 ⊗

Jl Kajeng

23 ⊗

UBUD KAJA

Museum Puri Lukisan

3 ◎
24 ⊗

34 ✪

33 ✪

39 🛍

SAMBAHAN

Campuan Ridge Walk

Sungai Wos

Sungai Cerik

CAMPUAN

Jl Raya Campuan

Neka Art Museum
4 ◎

28 ⊗

Bali Botanica Day Spa

10 ◎

14 ⊗

17 ⊗

Jl Raya Sanggingan

Sungai Blangsuh

Blanco Renaissance Museum
6 ◎

15 ⊗

Jl Raya Penestanan

Intuitive Flow
11 ◎

Jl Raya Ubud

29 🔵

✖ 18

Jl Peliatan

🔆 36

E

Jl Sukma

38 🔵
✖ 19

Jl Suarga

Nur
12 ◎ Salon

PADANGTEGAL

Jl Jembawan

8 ◎ Yoga
Barn

Jl Raya Pengosekan

2 Agung Rai
◎ Museum
of Art

D

37 ✪

Jl Goutama

Jl Hanoman

44 🔵

13 ◎ Zen

45 🔵

40 🔵

Taksu ◎

9 ◎

42 ✖ 22
✖ 27 ◎
21 26
41 ✖
31 🔵

Jl Kaj...

43 🔵

Gang Beji

Casa Luna
7 ◎ Cooking
School

Jl Bism...

18 🔵
30

32 ✖ 16

**UBUD
KELOD**

Monkey Forest Rd
(Jl Wanara Wana)

25 ✖

🅿 1

Sacred
Monkey Forest
Sanctuary

C

Jl Nyuhbulan

B

Sungai Wos

**KATIK
LANTANG**

A

5

6

7

8

Experiences

Sacred Monkey Forest Sanctuary

PARK

1 ◉ Map p104, C7

Besides three evocative temples and moody, jungle-like forest, the main attraction here is the antics of a band of grey-haired and greedy long-tailed Balinese macaques, which are nothing like the innocent-looking doe-eyed monkeys on the brochures. They are ever-vigilant for handouts from passing tourists. (☏0361-971304; Monkey Forest Rd; adult/child 20,000/10,000Rp; ⏰8.30am-6pm)

Agung Rai Museum of Art

ART MUSEUM

2 ◉ Map p104, D8

The impressive ARMA complex is the only place in Bali to see the haunting works by influential German artist Walter Spies. It is housed in several traditional buildings set in gardens and also features works by Lempad, Affandi, Sadali, Hofker, Bonnet and Le Mayeur. The collection is well labelled in English. (ARMA; ☏0361-976659; www.armamuseum.com; Jl Raya Pengosekan; admission 30,000Rp; ⏰9am-6pm)

Ubud Palace

Museum Puri Lukisan ART MUSEUM

3 ⊙ Map p104, C4

Fine examples of all schools of Balinese art are shown at this excellent museum. It was in Ubud that the modern Balinese art movement started; where artists first began to abandon purely religious themes and court subjects for scenes of everyday life. Just look at the lush composition of *Balinese Market* by Anak Agung Gde Sobrat to see the vibrancy of local painting. (Museum of Fine Arts; ☎0361-975136; www.mpl-ubud.com; off Jl Raya Ubud; admission 20,000Rp; ⊙9am-5pm)

Neka Art Museum ART MUSEUM

4 ⊙ Map p104, B1

This private museum has an excellent and diverse collection; it's the best place to learn about the development of painting in Bali. Various areas are named for some of Ubud's most renowned painters, including Arie Smit and I Gusti Nyoman Lempad. Also look for works by Louise Koke, Miguel Covarrubias, Han Snel and Antonio Blanco. (☎0361-975074; www.museumneka.com; Jl Raya Sanggingan; adult/child 50,000Rp/free; ⊙9am-5pm Mon-Sat, noon-5pm Sun)

Ubud Palace PALACE

5 ⊙ Map p104, D4

Ubud's royal family still lives in this palace in the heart of town. In purely Balinese style, it has some ornate features and carving but is more comfortable family compound than grand retreat. Buck House it ain't, especially as you can wander around at will. Just to the north, **Pura Marajan Agung** (Jl Suweta) has one of the finest gates you'll find and is the private temple for the royal family. (cnr Jl Raya Ubud & Jl Suweta)

Blanco Renaissance Museum ART MUSEUM

6 ⊙ Map p104, B4

The picture of Antonio Blanco mugging with Michael Jackson says it all. His namesake Blanco Renaissance Museum captures the artist's theatrical spirit: he specialised in erotic art, illustrated poetry and playing the role of an eccentric artist à la Dali. He died in Bali in 1999, and his flamboyant home is now this museum. (☎0361-975502; Jl Raya Campuan; admission 60,000Rp; ⊙9am-5pm)

☑ Top Tip

Ubud Information

Bali's best visitor centre, **Ubud Tourist Information** (Yaysan Bina Wisata; Map p104, D4; ☎0361-973285; Jl Raya Ubud; ⊙8am-8pm) can answer most questions and has up-to-date information on ceremonies and traditional performances held in the area. Picking up the weekly schedule of performances is essential. Dance tickets are sold here and it often arranges transport to the outlying venues.

Casa Luna Cooking School

COOKING COURSE

7 Map p104, C5

There are regular cooking courses at Honeymoon Guesthouse. Half-day courses (300,000Rp) cover ingredients, cooking techniques and the cultural background of the Balinese kitchen (not all visit the market). (☎0361-973282; www.casalunabali.com; Honeymoon Guesthouse, JI Bisma)

ARMA

COURSE

The cultural powerhouse, ARMA (see 2 ⊙ Map p104, D8) offers classes in painting, woodcarving and batik. Other courses include Balinese history, Hinduism and architecture. (☎0361-976659; www.armamuseum.com; JI Raya Pengosekan; classes US$25-55; ⊙9am-6pm)

Yoga Barn

YOGA

8 ⊙ Map p104, D7

Listen for the serenity leeching out from these trees back near a river valley. The name exactly describes what you'll find – although this barn never needs shovelling. A huge range of classes in yoga and life-affirming offshoots are held through the week. (☎0361-070992; www.balispirit.com; off JI Raya Pengosekan; classes from 110,000Rp; ⊙7am-8pm)

Taksu

SPA

9 ⊙ Map p104, D5

Somewhat hidden yet still in the heart of Ubud, Taksu has a long and rather lavish menu of treatments as well as a strong focus on yoga. There are private rooms for couples massages, a healthy cafe and a range of classes. (☎0361-971490; www.taksuspa.com; JI Goutama; massages from 65,000Rp; ⊙9am-10pm; ☎)

Bali Botanica Day Spa

SPA

10 ⊙ Map p104, B1

Set beautifully on a lush hillside past little fields of rice and ducks, this spa offers a range of treatments including Ayurvedic ones. Like a good pesto, the herbal massage is popular. Will provide transport. (☎0361-976739; www.balibotanica.com; JI Raya Sanggingan; massage from 150,000Rp; ⊙9am-8pm)

Intuitive Flow

YOGA

11 ⊙ Map p104, A3

A lovely yoga studio up amid the rice fields – although just climbing the concrete stairs to get here from Campuan may make you too pooped to pop your yoga togs on. Workshops in healing arts. (☎0361-977824; www.intuitiveflow.com; Penestanan; yoga from 100,000Rp)

Nur Salon

SPA

12 ⊙ Map p104, D5

In a traditional Balinese compound filled with labelled medicinal plants; offers a long menu of straightforward spa and salon services, including a Javanese massage that takes two hours. (☎0361-975352; JI Hanoman 28; 1hr massage 155,000Rp; ⊙9am-8pm)

Understand

Spas, Yoga, Healers & More

Ubud brims with salons and spas where you can heal, pamper, rejuvenate or otherwise focus on your personal needs, physical and mental. The larger hotels and resorts all have in-house spas, which are often quite lavish. There are also all manner of independent spas, which range from the sybaritic to the no-nonsense. At the latter you may find that the pleasure comes well after the pain. In addition, Ubud is home to all manner of practitioners. You can get an idea of what's available by perusing the enormous bulletin board outside Bali Buddha (p111).

Yoga

Demand for yoga in Ubud seems virtually unquenchable. Fortunately there is a plethora of studios, instructors and classes available. Every March the **Bali Spirit Festival** (www.balispiritfestival.com) celebrates yoga, good living and spiritual health with concerts, seminars and classes.

Traditional Healers

Bali's traditional healers, known as *balian* (*dukun* on Lombok), play an important part in Bali's culture by treating physical and mental illness, removing spells and channelling information from the ancestors. Many are found in Ubud.

Consider the following before a visit:

▶ Your treatment will be very public and probably painful. It may include deep tissue massage, being poked with sharp sticks or having chewed herbs spat on you.

▶ English is rarely spoken.

▶ Dress respectfully (long trousers and a shirt, better yet a sarong and sash).

▶ Women should not be menstruating.

▶ Bring an offering into which you have tucked the consulting fee, which will range from 100,000Rp to 200,000Rp per person.

Finding a *balian* can take some work. Ask at your hotel, which can probably help with making an appointment.

Zen   SPA

13 Map p104, D7

Down a little lane, this spa has a good reputation. It offers body scrubs, 90-minute *mandi lulur* (Javanese body scrubs) and a spice bath, among myriad other pleasures. (📞0361-970976; www.zenbalispa.com; Jl Hanoman; 1hr massage from 100,000Rp; ⏱9am-8pm)

Eating

Mozaic   FUSION $$$

14 🍴 Map p104, B2

Chef Chris Salans oversees this much-lauded top-end restaurant. Fine French fusion cuisine features on a constantly changing seasonal menu that takes its influences from tropical Asia. Dine in an elegant garden or ornate pavilion. Choose from four

---

☑ Top Tip

Choosing Galleries

Ubud is dotted with galleries – every street and lane seems to have a place exhibiting artwork for sale. They vary enormously in the choice and quality of items on display. Often you will find local artists in the most unusual places, including your guesthouse. The best way to deal with the plethora of choice is just keep browsing during your Ubud sojourn, gradually sorting out what seems special and what's replicated at every other stall.

---

tastings menus, one of which is simply a surprise. (📞0361-975768; www.mozaic-bali.com; Jl Raya Sanggingan; menus from 700,000Rp; ⏱6-10pm Tue-Sun)

Bridges   FUSION $$$

15 🍴 Map p104, B4

The namesake bridges are right outside this multilevel restaurant with sweeping views of the gorgeous Sungai River gorge. You'll hear the rush of the water over rocks far below while you indulge in a top-end cocktail over the rocks or choose from the changing and complex menu of fusion fare. Nightly wine specials at happy hour are popular. (📞0361-970095; www.bridgesbali.com; Jl Campuan; meals US$15-35)

Three Monkeys   FUSION $$

16 🍴 Map p104, C6

Have a passionfruit-crush cocktail and settle back amid the rice field's frog symphony. Add the glow of tiki torches for a magical effect. By day there are sandwiches, salads and gelati. At night there's a fusion menu of Asian classics (the prawn rolls are a must), pasta and steaks. (Monkey Forest Rd; meals from 80,000Rp)

Warung Pulau Kelapa   INDONESIAN $

17 🍴 Map p104, B2

A newish place along the road from Campuan to Sanggingan, Kelapa has stylish takes on local classics. The surrounds are stylish as well: plenty of whitewash and antiques. Terrace

Inside Blanco Renaissance Museum (p107)

tables across the wide expanse of grass are best. (Jl Raya Sanggingan; dishes 15,000Rp-30,000Rp)

Mama's Warung INDONESIAN $

18 Map p104, E5

A real budget find among the bargain homestays of Tebesaya. Mama herself cooks up Indo classics that are spicy and redolent with garlic (the avocado salad, yum!). The freshly made peanut sauce for the satay is silky smooth. (Jl Sukma; dishes 10,000Rp-20,000Rp)

Bali Buddha HEALTH FOOD $

19 Map p104, E5

This breezy upper-floor place offers a full range of vegetarian *jamu* (health tonics), salads, tofu curries, savoury crepes, pizzas and gelati. It has a comfy lounging area and is candlelit at night. On the ground floor a market sells organic fruit and vegetables, wondrous blueberry muffins, breads and cookies. The bulletin board is packed with idiosyncratic Ubud notices. (Jl Jembawan 1; meals from 30,000Rp; 🖉)

Café des Artistes BELGIAN $$

20 Map p104, C4

In a quiet and cultured perch up off Jl Raya Ubud, the popular (read: book in high season) Café des Artistes serves Belgian-accented food, although the menu strays into France and Indonesia as well. There are also some amazing steaks. Local art is on display and the bar is refreshingly cultured. (☎0361-972706; Jl Bisma 9X; meals from 120,000Rp; ⊙noon-11am)

Cafe Havana   LATIN AMERICAN $$

21 ✗ Map p104, D5

All that's missing is Fidel. Actually, the decrepitude of its namesake city is also missing from this smart and stylish cafe on smart and stylish Dewi Sita. The menu boasts many a dish with Latin flair, such as tasty pork numbers, but expect surprises such as a crème brûlée oatmeal in the morning that simply astounds. (☎0361-972973; Jl Dewi Sita; meals from 60,000Rp)

Kafe Batan Waru   INDONESIAN $$

22 ✗ Map p104, D5

One of Ubud's best, this cafe serves consistently excellent Indonesian food. Tired of *mie goreng* made from instant noodles? With noodles made

Local Life
Ubud's Library

The **Pondok Pecak Library & Learning Centre** (Map p104, D5; ☎0361-976194; Monkey Forest Rd; ⊙9am-5pm Mon-Sat, 1-5pm Sun), on the east side of the football field, is a relaxed place with a children's book section, a pleasant reading area on the roof, a lending library and a range of cultural and language courses on offer. It's a good place to refill your water bottle rather than buy another.

fresh daily, this version celebrates a lost art. Western dishes include sandwiches and salads. Smoked duck (*bebek betutu*) and spit-roasted pig (*babi guling*) can be ordered in advance. (☎0361-977528; Jl Dewi Sita; meals from 50,000Rp)

Warung Ibu Oka   BALINESE $

23 ✗ Map p104, D4

Opposite Ubud Palace, you'll see lunchtime crowds waiting for one thing: the eponymous Balinese-style roast suckling pig. Line up and find a place under the shelter for one of the most authentic meals you'll have in Ubud. Order a *spesial* to get the best cut. Get there early to avoid the day-tripping bus tours. (Jl Suweta; meals 30,000Rp-50,000Rp; ⊙11am-4pm)

Casa Luna   INDONESIAN $$

24 ✗ Map p104, C4

Enjoy creative Indonesian-focused dishes like addictive bamboo skewers of minced seafood satay (try to pick out the dozen or so spices). Bread, pastries, cakes and more from its well-known bakery are also a must. The owner, Janet de Neefe, is the force behind the lauded **Ubud Writers & Readers Festival**. (☎0361-977409; Jl Raya Ubud; meals from 50,000Rp)

Coffee & Silver   CAFE $

25 ✗ Map p104, C6

Tapas and more substantial items make up the menu at this comfortable place with seating inside and

Understand
Ubud's Hero of the Year

Ubud has a long tradition of locals and expats working together for the greater good of Indonesians. Just look at the bulletin boards at Bali Buddha and Kafe and you'll see meetings and all manner of opportunities to get involved.

These selfless commitments got high-profile attention in 2011 when CNN named Ubud's Robin Lim as its 'Hero of the Year' from many contenders worldwide. Through her Bumi Sehat Foundation (www.bumisehatbali.org), Lim brings healthcare, prenatal services and birthing assistance to thousands of women on Bali and the Aceh province of Sumatra every year. It's an incredible commitment and it brings sorely needed services to women in villages who have no other access to such care.

out. Vintage photos of Ubud line the walls. Have a coffee and watch people strolling down to their fate with the monkeys in the forest. (📞0361-975354; Monkey Forest Rd; 🕙10am-midnight; snacks from 20,000Rp)

Juice Ja Cafe
CAFE $

26 🍴 Map p104, D5

Glass of spirulina? Dash of wheat grass with your papaya juice? Organic fruits and vegetables go into the food at this funky bakery-cafe. Little brochures explain the provenance of items like the organic cashew nuts. Enjoy the patio. (📞0361-971056; Jl Dewi Sita; snacks from 20,000Rp)

Tutmak Cafe
CAFE $

27 🍴 Map p104, D5

The breezy multilevel location here, facing both Jl Dewi Sita and the football field, is a popular place for a refreshing drink or a meal. Local com-

ers on the make huddle around their laptops plotting their next move. (Jl Dewi Sita; meals 30,000Rp-90,000Rp; 🛜)

Naughty Nuri's
BARBECUE $$

28 🍴 Map p104, B1

This legendary expat hangout packs 'em in for grilled steaks, ribs and burgers, even if all the chewing needed gets in the way of chatting. Thursday night grilled-tuna specials are ridiculously popular, making something of a party scene. Potent martinis are the real draw, as are the antics of the many regulars. (📞0361-977547; Jl Raya Sanggingan; meals from 80,000Rp)

Drinking

Jazz Café
LIVE MUSIC, BAR

29 🍷 Map p104, E5

Ubud's most popular nightspot (and that's not faint praise even though

A traditional masked dancer, Ubud

competition might be lacking), Jazz Café offers a relaxed atmosphere in a charming garden that features coconut palms and ferns. The menu offers a range of good Asian fusion food and you can listen to live music from Tuesday to Saturday after 7.30pm. The cocktail list is long. (Jl Sukma 2; ☺5pm–midnight)

Laughing Buddha
CAFE

30 Map p104, C6

More stylish than your average warung, this casual cafe serves excellent coffee and good Indonesian food aimed at the discriminating Western palate. But the real action is at night when there's regular live music that

packs 'em in and fills the street out front. (Monkey Forest Rd)

Lebong Cafe
BAR

31 Map p104, C5

Get up, stand up, stand up for your... reggae. This nightlife hub stays open at least until midnight, with live reggae and rock most nights. A few other places good for drinks are nearby. (Monkey Forest Rd)

Napi Orti
BAR

32 Map p104, C6

This upstairs place is your best bet for a late-night drink. Get boozy under the hazy gaze of Jim Morrison and

Sid Vicious. (Monkey Forest Rd; drinks from 12,000Rp; ☺noon-late)

Entertainment

Pura Dalem Ubud
TRADITIONAL DANCE

33 ⭐ Map p104, C4

At the west end of Jl Raya Ubud, this open-air venue has a flamelit carved-stone backdrop and in many ways is the most evocative place to see a dance performance. Watch for the Semara Ratih troupe. (Jl Raya Ubud)

Pura Taman Saraswati
TRADITIONAL DANCE

34 ⭐ Map p104, C4

The beauty of the setting may distract you from the dancers, although at night you can't see the lily pads and lotus flowers that are such an attraction by day. (Ubud Water Palace; Jl Raya Ubud)

Understand
Dance Troupes: Good & Bad

All dance groups on Ubud's stages are not created equal. You've got true artists with international reputations and then you've got some who really shouldn't quit their day jobs. If you're a Balinese dance novice, you shouldn't worry too much about this; just pick a venue and go.

But after a few performances, you'll start to appreciate the differences in talent, and that's part of the enjoyment. Clue: if the costumes are dirty, the orchestra seems particularly uninterested and you find yourself watching a dancer and saying 'I could do that', then the group is B-level.

Excellent troupes who regularly perform in Ubud include the following:

▶ **Semara Ratih** High-energy, creative Legong interpretations.

▶ **Gunung Sari** Legong dance; one of Bali's oldest and most respected troupes.

▶ **Semara Madya** Kecak dance; especially good for the hypnotic monkey chants.

▶ **Sekaa Gong Wanita Mekar Sari** An all-women Legong troupe from Peliatan.

▶ **Tirta Sari** Legong dance.

▶ **Sadha Budaya** Barong dance.

☑ Top Tip

Day Trip Delirium

As Ubud's popularity grows the number of daytrippers is proliferating. Unfortunately most are dumped by their overly large tour buses at the corner by the Art Market and they are left pondering hordes of vendors selling the same tat found everywhere else. It's easy to wander about aimlessly and wonder what all the fuss is about. Although Ubud is best experienced over a couple of days and nights, you can get a sense of the place by following our daylong stroll (p102), which covers some of Ubud's essential elements.

Ubud Palace   TRADITIONAL DANCE

Performances are held here almost nightly against a beautiful backdrop in the palace compound (see 5 ◉ Map p104, D4), with the carvings highlighted by torches. You'll see lots of locals peaking over walls and around corners to see the shows. (Jl Raya Ubud)

Ubud Wantilan   TRADITIONAL DANCE

35 ✪ Map p104, D4

The unadorned meeting *bale* across from Ubud Palace couldn't be easier to find. Get a Bintang from the ice buckets of one of the charming vendors and find a rickety plastic seat up front. (Jl Raya Ubud)

Puri Desa Gede   TRADITIONAL DANCE

36 ✪ Map p104, E8

A good, well-lit venue that regularly attracts some of Bali's best troupes. (Jl Peliatan)

Padangtegal Kaja   TRADITIONAL DANCE

37 ✪ Map p104, D5

A simple, open venue in a very convenient location. In many ways this location hints at what dance performances have looked like in Ubud for generations. (Jl Hanoman)

Shopping

Ganesha Bookshop   BOOKS

38 🔒 Map p104, E5

Ubud's best bookshop has an amazing amount of stock jammed into a small space; an excellent selection of titles on Indonesian studies, travel, arts, music, fiction (including used titles) and maps. Good staff recommendations. (www.ganeshabooksbali.com; Jl Raya Ubud)

Threads of Life Indonesian Textile Arts Center   TEXTILES

39 🔒 Map p104, D3

This small store is part of a foundation that works to preserve traditional textile creation in Balinese villages. There's a small but visually stunning collection of exquisite handmade fabrics in stock. (Jl Kajeng 24)

Goddess on the Go!
WOMEN'S CLOTHING

40 🔒 Map p104, D8

Women's clothes for adventure. Super-comfortable, easy-to-pack and made eco-friendly. There's a lot of selection in this large store. (Jl Raya Pengosekan)

Kertas Gingsir
GIFTS

41 🔒 Map p104, D5

This cute little place specialises in gorgeous and heavily textured papers handmade from banana, pineapple and taro plants. If you're into pulp, ask about factory visits as everything is made near Ubud. (Jl Dewi Sita)

Kou
GIFTS

42 🔒 Map p104, D5

Luxurious locally handmade organic soaps perfume your nose as you enter. Put one in your undies drawer and smell fine for weeks. The range is un-like that found in chain stores selling luxe soap. (Jl Dewi Sita)

Macan Tidur
ART & ANTIQUES

43 🔒 Map p104, C5

Amid a string of trashy places selling tourist tat, this elegant store stands out like Audrey Hepburn amid the Spice Girls. Silks, art, antiques and more are beautifully displayed in a lovely shop that will have you pondering your shipping options. (Monkey Forest Rd)

Namaste
NEW AGE

44 🔒 Map p104, D7

Just the place to buy a crystal to get your spiritual house in order, Namaste is a gem of a little store with a top range of New Age supplies. Incense, yoga mats, moody instrumental music – it's all here. (Jl Hanoman 64)

Pondok Bamboo
MUSIC

45 🔒 Map p104, D7

Hear the music of a thousand bamboo wind chimes at this shop owned by noted gamelan musician Nyoman Warsa. Gamelans in many forms are on offer and the master himself is ready to explain the workings. Ask about the regular puppet and music performances. (Monkey Forest Rd)

Pasar Seni
SOUVENIRS

46 🔒 Map p104, D4

Many bus-bound tourists can feel trapped at this chaotic warren of stalls in the heart of Ubud. Clothing, sarongs, footwear and souvenirs of highly variable quality (the penis-shaped bottle openers are top sellers) are sold at highly negotiable prices. Take our advice and steer clear, using your time exploring nearby streets. (Art Market; Jl Raya Ubud)

Explore

East Bali

Some of the lushest land in Bali is found in the east. Ancient rice terraces spill down the sides of hills into wide river valleys. Long beaches in the west give way to smaller hidden ones in the east. Padangbai is a port town with a funky feel while Semarapura has important relics from Bali's royal past.

The Region in a Day

☀ East Bali makes a splendid daytrip from both south Bali and Ubud. Start your day watching for the towering Gunung Agung, the island's most sacred volcano. Clouds usually obscure it in the heat of the day. While it's still cool, drive the **Sidemen Road** (p121) and maybe stop for a rice field ramble. Or you might plunge into the family fun of **Bali Safari & Marine Park** (p121).

☼ For lunch, try one of the choices along the coast road such as local fave **Merta Sari** (p122) or the fabulous fare and luxe surrounds of **Amankila Terrace** (p122). After lunch, take time at a beach such as **Pasir Putih** (p122) or one of the many black-sand beaches towards Sanur. Wander historic **Semarapura** (p121) and **Taman Kertha Gosa** (p123); check out the local markets.

☾ Daytrippers will want to be back home by dark. But if you're staying, **Padangbai** (p121) has a mellow beach vibe mixed with a groovy traveller charm; otherwise, resorts and hotels great and small are scattered along the coast and near Sidemen.

 Best of Bali

Snorkelling
Padangbai (p121)

Beaches
Lebih Beach (p121)

Pasir Putih (p121)

Eating
Gianyar Babi Guleng (p122)

For Kids
Bali Safari & Marine Park (p121)

Getting There & Around

🚗 **Car** From south Bali or Ubud you can arrange a car and driver for about US$50 per day to go touring in the east.

Walk Within Semarapura and Pandangbai you can easily walk between sights. However, you'll need transport to get from one part to another of this large region.

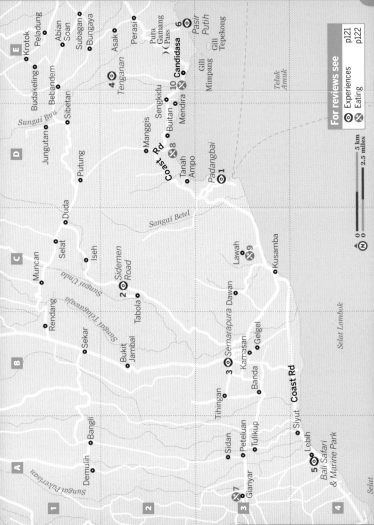

E

Krotok
Peladung
Abian Soan
Subagan
Bungaya

Asak
Perasi

Pura Gamang Pass
6 Pasir Putih
Gili Tepekong

Budakeling
Bebandem
Sibetan

4 Tenganan
Gili Mimpang

Candidasa
10 ⊗
Teluk Amuk

Sungai Buru
Jungutan
Putung

Manggis
Sengkidu
Buitan
Mendira

D

Coast Rd
8 ⊗
Tanah Ampo.

Padangbai
1 ◉

Teluk Amuk

5 km
2.5 miles
0
0
N

Duda
Selat
Iseh

Sangai Betel

C

Muncan

2 ◉ Sidemen Road

Lawah
9 ⊗

Kusamba

Rendang
Sekar

Bukit Jambal
Tabola

Sungai Telagawaja
Sungai Unda

Dawan
Semarapura

Selat Lombok

B

3 ◉ Semarapura
Kamasan
Gelgel

Banda

Tihingan

Coast Rd

Bangli

Sidan
Peteluan
Tulikup

Syiut

Lebih
5 ◉ Bali Safari & Marine Park

A

Sungai Pakerisan

Demulih

7 ⊗
Gianyar

Selat

3

1   **2**   **3**   **4**

Experiences

Padangbai TOWN

1 Map p120, D3

Bali's eastern port city makes a good base for exploration. You can relax on the beach with a beer while watching the Lombok ferry come and go or head just over a knoll to the light-sand Blue Lagoon Beach, which is a good place to snorkel. The cool traveller vibe makes this a good choice for an overnight stop.

Sidemen Road SCENIC DRIVE

2 ◉ Map p120, C2

Sidemen has a spectacular location and the road that runs through it may be the most beautiful in Bali (start at Semarapura, end near Duda). There are many walks through the rice fields and streams in the multihued green valley that forms what could be an amphitheatre for the gods. Little guesthouses sit amid the splendour.

Semarapura TOWN

3 ◉ Map p120, B3

Besides its history (see p123), Semara- pura is a good place to stroll and get a feel for modern Balinese life. The mar- kets are large and offer a vast range of Balinese goods, yet a dearth of tourists keeps the mood authentic. Glittery gold shops vie with plastic emporiums for shoppers' attention; a profusion of fruit is everywhere.

Tenganan VILLAGE

4 ◉ Map p120, E2

Bali's oldest inhabitants are the Bali Aga people, who lead lives separate from Hindu Bali. Tenganan, their spir- itual home, is surrounded by a wall, which protects the small village from outside influences. Not *all* outside influences, mind you, as the Aga have found profits in accepting visitors, al- beit quite gently. Tenganan is 4km off the coast road just west of Candidasa.

Bali Safari & Marine Park AMUSEMENT PARK

5 ◉ Map p120, A4

Kids love this animal theme park. Displays are large and naturalistic; camel and elephant rides are popular. The vast park is north of Lebih Beach. The Bali Agung Shows take Balinese culture and give it a lavish Vegas treatment. (☎0361-950000; www. balisafarimarinepark.com; Prof Dr Ida Bagus

◯ Local Life
Bali's Eastern Beaches

The busy coast road from Sanur going east makes it easy to get to scores of beaches. The grey sands are mostly empty and the surf is al- ways treacherous. A couple of good choices are **Saba Beach** (Map p120, A4), which has a small temple, and **Lebih Beach** (Map p120, A4), which has sand filled with mica that spar- kles with a billion points of light.

Mantra Bypass; admission adult/child from US$49/39; ⏰9am-5pm)

Pasir Putih
BEACH

6 ◉ Map p120, E2

The name of this idyllic white-sand beach backed by coconut trees indeed means 'White Sand'. Simple thatched cafes offer snacks and cold Bintangs. Access is an adventure: 5.6km east of Candidasa, follow a pretty paved track off the main road for 1.5km to a temple, where locals will collect a fee. The beach is another 600m down a very bad road.

Eating

Gianyar Babi Guleng
BALINESE $

7 🍴 Map p120, A3

People come to Gianyar to sample the market food, like the *babi guling* (spit-roast pig stuffed with chilli, turmeric, garlic and ginger). Although scoring a zero for imagination in naming it, this open-air shopfront scores a 10 for its *babi,* which is first among much competition. It's on a tiny side street at the west end of the centre. (Gianyar; meals from 20,000Rp; ⏰7am-4pm)

Amankila Terrace
FUSION $$$

8 🍴 Map p120, D2

One of Bali's finest hotels is hidden along the jutting cliffs about 5km beyond the Padangbai turn-off. The renowned architecture includes three pools that step down to the sea in matching shades of a blue. Above

Meet an owl at Bali Safari & Marine Park (p121)

this beauty, the superb Terrace is the resort's casual cafe and has a creative menu showing global and local influences. (☎0363-41333; www.amankila.com; Manggis; meals from US$15; ⏰8am-5pm)

Merta Sari
INDONESIAN $$

9 🍴 Map p120, C3

Follow the crowds of Balinese to this open-air pavilion that's famous for its *nasi campur.* This version of the island's plate lunch includes juicy, pounded fish satay, a slightly sour, fragrant fish broth, fish steamed in banana leaves, snake beans in a fragrant tomato-peanut sauce and a fiery red sambal. Merta Sari is 300m north of the coast road in Bingin. Look for the signs. (Bingin; meals from 25,000Rp; ⏰10am-3pm)

Understand

Semarapura & Bali's History

From the 14th to the 16th centuries, Gegel, a town very close to today's Semarapura, was the centre of power on Bali. In the 1700s, however, internal squabbling diluted the local royalty's influence, and royals from other parts of Bali vied for power.

Still, in 1849 the rulers of Klungkung (which had superseded Gegel as the royal centre and is today called Semarapura) and Gianyar defeated a Dutch invasion force at Kusamba. Before the Dutch could launch a counter-attack, a force from Tabanan arrived and the trader Mads Lange was able to broker a peace settlement.

The Suicidal Last Stand

For the next 50 years the south Bali kingdoms squabbled, until the rajah of Gianyar petitioned the Dutch for support. When the Dutch finally invaded the south, the king of Klungkung had a choice between a suicidal *puputan,* like the rajah of Denpasar, or an ignominious surrender, as Tabanan's rajah had done. He chose the former. In April 1908, as the Dutch surrounded his palace, Taman Kertha Gosa, the Dewa Agung and hundreds of his relatives and followers marched out to certain death from Dutch gunfire or the blades of their own kris (traditional daggers). Klungkung – today called Semarapura – was the last Balinese kingdom to succumb and the sacrifice is commemorated in the large Puputan Monument. Locals still have great pride in the toughness of their ancestors.

Taman Kertha Gosa

This **palace** (adult/child 12,000/6000Rp, parking 2000Rp; ⏱7am-6pm) was established in 1710 when the Dewa Agung dynasty moved to today's Semarapura from nearby Gegel. It was laid out as a large square, believed to be in the form of a mandala, with courtyards, gardens, pavilions and moats. Most of the original palace and grounds were destroyed by Dutch attacks in 1908 – the elaborately carved gateway on the south side of the square is all that remains of the palace itself. However, the Kertha Gosa, the old royal court, survives and is a splendid example of open-air Balinese architecture. While wandering the gardens, save time for the good little museum.

Top Experiences
Gili Trawangan

Getting There

🚤 **Boat** Gili Cat
(📞0361-271680;
www.gilicat.com)
leaves from Padang-
bai; Blue Water
Express (📞0361-310
4558; www.bwsbali
.com) leaves from near
Tanjung Benoa. Rates
are US$70 one way.

Gili Trawangan's main drag boasts a glittering roster of lounge bars, hip hotels and cosmopolitan restaurants, mini-marts and dive schools. And yet behind this glitzy facade, a bohemian character endures, with rickety warungs and reggae joints surviving between the cocktail tables. Fast boats have brought Gili T close to Bali, and, for many, a night or two partying here – with maybe some day time in the beautiful waters – is an essential part of their trip.

Snorkel boat at Gili Trawangan

Don't Miss

Beaches

Gili T is almost ringed with sand, and on the east side of the island – where most of the action is – this sand is among the nicest in Indonesia. Think pearly white grains lapped by azure blue waters and you get the scene.

Snorkelling

Ringed by coral reefs and with easy beach access, Gili T offers superb snorkelling. If you enjoy swimming, there's no better feeling than exploring a reef without the burden of a tank on your back. You can start on any beach or go further out on one of many glass-bottomed boats. Besides the many fish, it's common to see sea turtles.

Diving

The Gili Islands are a superb dive destination as the marine life is plentiful and varied. Turtles and black- and white-tip reef sharks are common, and the macro life is excellent, with sea horses, pipefish and lots of crustaceans. Around the full moon large schools of bumphead parrotfish appear to feast on coral spawn; at other times manta rays cruise past dive sites.

Nightlife

Gili T morphs between rave-up central and boutique chic. Parties are held three nights a week (Monday, Wednesday and Friday), shifting between venues. DJs mix house, trance and increasingly some r 'n' b as the scene gets more commercial. The island has more than a dozen great beachside drinking dens, ranging from sleek lounge bars to simple shacks.

☑ Top Tips

▶ Gili T's neighbours, Gili Meno and Gili Air, are much quieter, with a fraction of Gili T's nightlife.

▶ There are fly-by-night boat operators to the Gilis and there have been accidents; stick with the experienced companies.

▶ Gili Trawangan has a couple of ATMs and foreign cards are accepted.

▶ During Ramadan, nightlife is curtailed out of respect for local culture.

✖ Take a Break

Enjoying a prime beachfront location, **Scallywags** (meals 40,000-100,000Rp; 🛜) has tables under Arabian-style canvas and an attractive shabby-chic interior. Specials are chalked up daily on blackboards. The menu has everything from freshly grilled fish to pasta, panini and wraps to 'Full Monty' breakfasts.

The Best of
Bali

Surfboards for hire in Legian (p22)
KYLIE MCLAUGHLIN/LONELY PLANET IMAGES ©

Best Walks
Ayung River Valley

🏃 The Walk

The wonders of the Ayung River (Sungai Ayung) are the focus of this outing, which may be close to Ubud but are a world away in terms of pure tropical splendour. You'll walk in a lush valley past a rushing river amid impossibly green vistas. Along the way you'll pass through an iconically typical village and you'll cross through the old compound of one of Bali's greatest expat writers.

Start Campuan bridge

Finish Campuan bridge

Length 5km; five hours

🍴 Take a Break

There are no breaks in the valley! Bring plenty of water and assemble a picnic from a deli or cafe in Ubud. But towards the end of your walk, options abound for a pause. The cafes line up like a string of oases as you make your way blessedly downhill on Jl Raya Sanggingan.

Lush Sayan

❶ Penestanan

From the Campuan bridge, climb the steep concrete stairs opposite the Hotel Tjampuhan and walk west past rice fields and artists' studios to the village of **Penestanan**. You'll see artists' studios and traditional family compounds. Look for the small temple that always graces a corner.

❷ Sayan

Now head north on a small road that curves around to **Sayan** and the **Sayan Terrace hotel**. This was the site of Colin McPhee's home in the 1930s, as chronicled in his excellent book *A House in Bali* (available at island bookshops). He was one of the first Westerners to take a scholarly approach to documenting Bali's music and dance.

❸ Path into the Valley

Follow the downhill path before the gate to the hotel's rooms. It's steep and can be slippery, plus there are offshoots that can lead you astray; locals will help you find your way down for a tip of 10,000Rp.

❹ Ayung River Valley

Following the rough trails north, along the eastern side of the **Ayung**, you traverse steep slopes, cross paddy fields and pass irrigation canals through dense tropical jungle. You don't need to follow any specific trail as you head slowly north along the river. Water plunges over huge boulders and eddies in cool-looking pools.

❺ Kedewatan

After about 1.5km of meandering through the river valley (take your time, wander about, see what you discover) you'll reach the finish point for white-water rafting trips that start further upriver. Under a dense canopy of trees, take a good but steep trail up to the main road at **Kedewatan**; head north then east about 1 km along the main road into Ubud.

❻ Sanggingan

At **Sanggingan** the road curves 90 degrees due south and begins the long, gentle descent to the Campuan bridge where you started. Among the many cafes along here, you might feel you deserve one of the famous martinis at Naughty Nuri's, or you can stop at the Neka Art Museum to see how artists portrayed many of the sights you've seen.

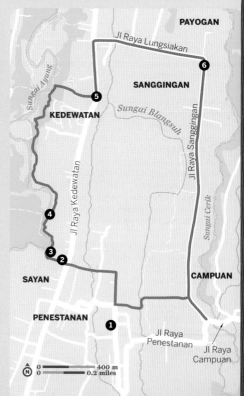

Best
Beaches

Bali is ringed with beaches, which is one of the reasons all those planes keep landing at the airport. They come in so many forms that there's virtually a beach for everyone. There's a reason that tourism started in Kuta: just look at that beach. It disappears in both directions and has ceaselessly crashing waves, which at their best are long aqua ribbons twisting into white.

A Beach for Any Mood

On Sundays Kuta Beach is thronged with locals; on any day massage women languidly ply their trade while men offer up cheap beers from coolers. Vacationers claim a part of the beach they like, make friends with the vendors and return to 'their' beach for the rest of their trip.

From Seminyak north through Batubelig and on to Echo Beach, hipster hangouts vie with posh clubs and humble beer vendors for business. South of the airport, the vast arid rock that is the Bukit Peninsula shelters a score of beaches hidden in small coves below the cliffs all the way to Ulu Watu. Coming closest to the white-sand cliché, these idylls are good for watching the world-class surfing offshore amid beautiful surrounds.

Meanwhile, in Nusa Dua, Tanjung Benoa and Sanur families frolic on mellow reef-sheltered beaches picked clean daily. East Bali has a swath of seldom-visited volcanic black-sand beaches while Nusa Lembongan has funky beach guesthouses with awesome sunset views. Over on Gili T, the sand is white and lined with bars and clubs for a full-on party scene.

☑ Top Tips

▶ Although Bali's west-facing beaches from Echo Beach to Ulu Watu offer spectacular sunsets, east-facing ones like Sanur enjoy their own show as Nusa Lembongan and the islands glow pink offshore.

▶ Almost every beach has at least one vendor ready to pull a cold one out of the cooler.

Lazy days on Balangan Beach (p69)

Best for Hanging with Friends

Double Six Beach (p26) Fun mix of visitors and locals.

Gili Trawangan (p124) Those raves about the raves are just the start.

Seminyak Beach (p37) Clubs and cafes great and humble dot the sand.

Batubelig Beach (p49) The new hotspot with a swath of groovy beach bars and cafes.

Balangan Beach (p69) Classic cove beach is worth the drive.

Kuta Beach (p26) The original beach still knows how to kick up some sand.

Echo Beach (p49) Gnarly surf action entertains the masses.

Padang Padang Beach (p69) Small enough to be one big scene on busy days.

Jungutbatu Beach (p91) The funky surfer vibe never goes out of style.

Pasir Putih (p122) The coolest beach in East Bali has cooler cafes.

Best for Families

Sanur Beach (p85) Reefs offshore keep the surf mellow, just like the town.

Mushroom Bay (p91) Small resorts, water sports and a surf-protected site.

Best for Escaping

Pantai Nelayan (p57) No easy access makes this the spot not to be spotted.

Lebih Beach (p121) The sparkles in the black sand outnumber visitors a trillion to one.

Best **Nightlife**

The nightclubs of Kuta, Legian and Seminyak are one of Bali's biggest draws. The partying starts at beachside bars at sunset and moves to an ever-changing line-up of bars and clubs. Bouncing from one to another all night long is a Bali tradition that guarantees you'll be over-heated from the exertion, the mixes, the booze, the companionship or all of the above.

Nightlife for Every Taste

You can quaff an ice-cold Bintang at sandy-floored bars with the full tropical cliché. At the other end of the style spectrum there are posh scenester clubs where you'll spend more time prepping your killer look in advance than actually partying.

Mostly, however, nights on Bali are lacking in rules or pretension: on any night you can listen to live rock, dance salsa, see a drag show, get lost in the groove of a famous DJ, win (or lose) a shot contest or just have a smashing good time with friends new and old.

IGNACIO PALACIOS/LONELY PLANET IMAGES ©

☑ Top Tip

▶ Enjoying traditional Balinese nightlife may be the best memory of your trip: the dance performances in and around Ubud combine beauty, talent, drama and even comedy.

Best Partying

Sky Garden Lounge (p31) Floor after floor of club and bar action fuelled by drink specials.

Bounty (p32) So lowbrow it's a must.

Gili Trawangan (p124) The entire island is renowned for its all-night raving clubbing.

Best Stylish Drinking

Potato Head (p41) High-concept lounge and cocktails on the Seminyak sands.

Red Carpet Champagne Bar (p41) Ridiculously over-the-top for fizzy drinks and oysters.

Best Live Music

Jazz Café (p113) Regular live acts belie the rumour that Ubud has no nightlife.

Bali Jo (p42) Bali's best drag shows.

JP's (p41) An everchanging line-up of live music in a cool yet mellow club.

Best
Pampering

Whether it's a total fix for the mind, body and spirit, or simply the desire for some quick-fix serenity, lots of travellers in Bali are spending hours and days being massaged, scrubbed, perfumed, pampered, bathed and blissed-out. Sometimes this happens on the beach or in a garden, other times you'll find yourself in stylish, even lavish surroundings.

PAUL KENNEDY/LONELY PLANET IMAGES ©

Bliss in Every Flavour

Spas may be serious or they may seem frivolous, they can be found down little lanes or in the most exclusive hotels. Treatments are myriad, from the almost sensually relaxing to serious endeavours designed to purge your body and maybe your soul of toxins. You can lie back and enjoy or take active part; yoga is hugely popular. Happily the Balinese have just the right cultural background and disposition to enhance the experience.

Balinese Massage

Traditional Balinese massage techniques of stretching, long strokes, skin rolling and palm and thumb pressure result in a lowering of tension, improved blood flow and circulation, and an all-over feeling of calm. Traditional herbal treatments are popular.

Best Massage

Jari Menari (p37) Bali's renowned centre for serious massage.

Garbugar (p26) Skilled blind masseurs are the locals' choice.

Best Pampering Spa

Prana (p37) Utterly lavish in its treatments and opulent in décor.

Amanusa Spa (p79) Sets the standard for resort spas.

Jamu Traditional Spa (p86) Popular, serene and posh.

Bali Botanica Day Spa (p108) A little quirky, a little creative, just like Ubud.

Best Yoga

Yoga Barn (p108) *The* centre for all things yoga in Ubud.

Taksu (p108) Combines yoga with spa treatments.

Desa Seni (p49) The south Bali choice for serious yoga.

Best for Cleansing Your Body

Ubud Sari Health Resort (p102) Purge yourself of your excesses.

Best
Diving &
Snorkelling

Having a 3m-long sunfish stare at you is reason enough to go diving on Bali. These huge creatures are found at many spots around Bali, as are a huge variety of other fish and mammals, from parrotfish to whales. And snorkelling, at spots all around the islands, can be just as rewarding.

T.M. ROCK/LONELY PLANET IMAGES ©

Diving Bali

With its warm water, extensive coral reefs and abundant marine life, Bali offers excellent diving adventures. Reliable dive schools and operators all around Bali's coasts can train complete beginners or arrange challenging trips that will satisfy the most experienced divers. Out on Nusa Lembongan, you'll find top-notch dive operators who can take you to sites there and at neighbouring Nusa Penida – a world-class dive location. Gili T provides equally excellent opportunities.

If you are not picky, you'll find all the equipment you need (the quality, size and age of the equipment can vary). If you provide your own, you can usually get a discount on your dive. Some small, easy-to-carry things to bring from home include protective gloves, spare straps, silicone lubricant and extra globes/bulbs for your torch/flashlight.

Snorkelling Bali

Snorkelling gear is available near all the most accessible spots, but if you're keen, it's definitely worthwhile bringing your own and checking out some of the less-visited parts of the coasts. Anywhere there's a reef, you won't go wrong slipping into the water to see what else is swimming around.

☑ Top Tips

▶ Ask to see dive operators' certificates or certification cards – no reputable shop will be offended by this request. To guide certified divers on a reef dive, guides must hold at least 'rescue diver' or preferably 'dive master' qualifications.

▶ At a minimum, a dive boat should carry oxygen and a first-aid kit. A radio or mobile phone is also important.

Diving the blue lagoons of Bali

Best Diving

Pulau Menjangan (p135)
A 30m-wall is one of the highlights at Bali's best dive spot.

Gili Trawangan (p124)
Dive shops and spots abound on Gili T. Free-diving is popular here, and there are reefs in all directions.

Nusa Lembongan (p90)
There are dozens of great sites here and at the two neighbouring islands.

World Diving (p91)
Excellent Nusa Lembongan operator leads trips and offers certification. It also organises trips to the deep and challenging waters off nearby Nusa Penida.

Crystal Divers (p85)
Sanur's top dive shop gives great lessons and organises trips.

Best Snorkelling

Pulau Menjangan (p135)
It's not just diving: let the current carry you over extraordinary beauty.

Gili Trawangan (p124)
Wander into water teeming with fish and reefs right off the beach.

Nusa Lembongan (p90)
Reefs and mangroves combine for many fine sites.

Padangbai (p121)
Nearby beach coves have fun snorkelling right off the beach.

Surya Water Sports (p86) Sanur's best water-sports shop offers boat trips for snorkellers.

Worth a Trip

Pulau Menjangan is Bali's best-known dive area and has a dozen superb dive sites. The diving is excellent – iconic tropical fish, soft corals, great visibility (usually), caves and a spectacular drop-off. It's located on the northwest coast of the island and is best visited as part of an overnight jaunt to Pemuteran, which has resorts.

Best
Eating

Fusion cooking is the hallmark of inventive menus found across south Bali and Ubud. Creative chefs take techniques and influences from across the globe and combine them into menus that surprise and delight. On a list of reasons to visit Bali, the food – from humble Balinese to extravagantly global – must always be included.

LYNN GAIL/LONELY PLANET IMAGES ©

Balinese Food

Balinese food is pungent and lively. The biting note of fresh ginger is matched by the heat of raw chillies, shrimp paste, palm sugar and tamarind. There is nothing shy about this cuisine.

You can taste South Indian, Malaysian and Chinese flavours in Balinese food. It has evolved from years of cross-cultural cook-ups and trading with sea-faring pioneers, and perhaps even pirates, across the seas of Asia.

Don't miss lunch at a warung, where you choose from an array of dishes that can be mixed and matched to your stomach's content. Spicy, vegetarian, nuanced, meaty, seafood, it's all here along with a choice of several kinds of rice.

Casual Fare

For a cuisine that is so nuanced, it may surprise that more often than not it is simply wolfed down. The Western idea of coming together doesn't apply to the Balinese, who eat when they are hungry. Gatherings involving food are saved for ceremonies and festivals. Rather, Balinese meals are most often cooked by vendors, whether manning a roaring wok, pushing a cart (the ultimate convenience food) or slaving away all morning so that hordes can descend at lunch and lay waste to dozens of warung dishes.

☑ **Top Tips**

▶ Plunge into any Balinese food market and buy any fruit that looks unfamiliar. It costs little and tastes amazing.

▶ Much of the heat in Balinese food comes from the sambal. Ask for extra (not the commercial bottled stuff, the handmade kind) and earn respect – and enjoyment.

Best Top End

Sardine (p50) Beautiful food in a beautiful setting.

Mozaic (p110) Creativity mixed with lavish fare from an ambitious kitchen.

Satay, market-style

Bumbu Bali (p80) An exquisite night out sampling the best the island offers.

Bridges (p110) Fine fusion fare with gorgeous Ubud views.

Sarong (p52) Flavours from across Asia meet in a magical setting.

Best Local

Warung Sulawesi (p55) Defines tasty Balinese warung fare.

Warung Pulau Kelapa (p110) Dishes from across Indonesia served with colour and flair.

Warung Sobat (p52) Fresh seafood served in the simplest possible ways.

Gianyar Babi Guleng (p122) A superb source of Bali's signature dish.

Best Casual

Biku (p38) One of the island's most popular restaurants never hits a wrong note.

Three Monkeys (p110) Long-running pan-Asian fave in Ubud on a rice field.

Teba Mega Cafe (p63) The best of myriad choices for Jimbaran seafood.

Warung Soba (p103) The definitive New Agey Ubud restaurant is healthy and tasty.

Made's Warung II (p39) An old fave for Asian food has been reinvigorated.

Waroeng Bonita (p52) Tasty fare in a garden venue with occasional drag shows.

Indiana Kenanga (p91) Complex and skilful dishes out on isolated Nusa Lembongan.

Best
Surfing

PAUL KENNEDY/LONELY PLANET IMAGES ©

Listen to the accents of the surfers: Australian, American, Italian, Dutch, Japanese, Balinese (yes, lots of Balinese!) and many more are heard. People from all over the world come to Bali to surf, which shouldn't surprise anyone. Bali's surf breaks are legend and they are many. The series off Ulu Watu are among the world's best.

Where to Surf

Swells come from the Indian Ocean, so the surf is on the southern side of the island and, strangely, on the northwest coast of Nusa Lembongan, where the swell funnels into the strait between there and the Bali coast.

In the dry season (around April to September) the west coast, from Ulu Watu to Echo Beach and beyond, has the best breaks; this is also when Nusa Lembongan works best. In the wet season surf the eastern side of the island.

South Bali has myriad surf schools, and when it comes time to don the look, there are entire retail empires owned by people who were once just surfers, dude.

Best Surf Breaks

Kuta Beach (p26) Bali's original surf beach is still a winner.

Double Six Beach (p26) Great mix of tourists and locals.

Echo Beach (p49) Wild waves and plenty of spectators.

Ulu Watu (p72) Bali's best surf breaks are truly incredible.

Balangan (p71) Right off a great beach with fun cafes.

Bingin (p71) Close to cheap surfer dives, this isolated beach is worth the climb down a cliff.

Impossibles (p71) Somewhat isolated, for when you don't want an audience.

Nusa Lembongan (p91) Three famous breaks are right off Jungutbatu Beach.

Best Surf Schools

Pro Surf School (p26) Long-running school that can get almost anyone surfing.

Rip Curl School of Surf (p26) Part of an entire surfing lifestyle empire.

Best for Kids

Bali is a good place for kids. There are lots of fun and frolic, and the locals are especially enamoured of pint-sized visitors. Cool things to do include beaches, pools (almost every hotel has one), mysterious temples, monkeys, tourist parks geared to kids, ocean adventures like snorkelling, and a lot more.

WIBOWO RUSLI/LONELY PLANET IMAGES ©

The Balinese & Children

To the Balinese, children are considered part of the community and everyone, not just the parents, has a responsibility towards them. Little ones are a social asset when you travel and people will display great interest in any Western child they meet. Key kid details in Bahasa Indonesia: *bulau* (month), *tahun* (year), *laki-laki* (boy) and *perempuan* (girl).

Best Watery Fun

Rip Curl School of Surf (p26) Popular surf school has kids' programs.

Benoa Marine Recreation (p80) Oodles of aquatic fun.

Sanur Beach (p85) Mellow waters and lots of clean sand.

Surya Water Sports (p86) Tons of cool reasons to get wet.

Mushroom Bay (p91) Sheltered beach on Nusa Lembongan with water sports.

Best Amusement Parks

Bali Safari & Marine Park (p121) Wild animals, shows, rides and more.

Waterbom Park (p27) A wet, wild and watery kingdom.

Best Random Fun

Sacred Monkey Forest Sanctuary (p106) Indiana Jones temples in a forest filled with monkeys.

Pura Luhur Ulu Watu (p71) An ancient temple

☑ Top Tips

▶ Look for beach vendors selling kites; huge breezy fun.

▶ An hour north of Ubud, **Elephant Safari Park** (www.baliadventuretours.com) is home to retired logging elephants from other parts of Indonesia. No one can resist a ride.

with sea views and, yes, monkeys.

Fruit Market (p53) Fruits like no Western kid has ever seen.

JJ Bali Button (p54) Millions of cool buttons.

Bali Kite Festival (p89) Ginormous kites roaring overhead.

Best
Shopping

Bali's shops could occupy days of your holiday. Designer boutiques (Bali has a thriving fashion industry), funky stores, slick galleries, wholesale emporiums and family-run workshops are just some of the choices. The shopping scene is like a form of primordial soup. New boutiques appear, old ones vanish, some change into something else while others move up the food chain.

TOM COCKREM / LONELY PLANET IMAGES ©

Bargaining

Price tags only make sporadic appearances in Bali's stores. Most everyday purchases require bargaining. A certain price flexibility even applies at many of Seminyak's trendiest boutiques. (The only certain exceptions are international chains, but why bother in the first place?)

Although visitors used to forking over the total shown on the scanner may be intimidated by the need to negotiate, bargaining can be an enjoyable part of shopping in Bali. Keep your sense of humour, and remember the old bromide 'why pay retail?'.

Bargaining Tips

▶ Have some idea what the item is worth.

▶ Establish a starting price – ask the seller for their price rather than making an initial offer.

▶ Your first price can be from one-third to two-thirds of the asking price – assuming that the asking price is not outrageous.

▶ With offers and counter-offers, move closer to an acceptable price.

▶ If you don't get to an acceptable price, you're entitled to walk – the vendor may call you back with a lower price.

▶ Note that when you name a price, you're committed – you must buy if your offer is accepted.

▶ Don't push if the prices really are set.

☑ Top Tips

▶ Much of Kuta, Legian and certain euphemistically named 'art markets' in Ubud, Seminyak and elsewhere are filled with junk that's not even made on Bali.

▶ The top-selling souvenir is the penis-shaped bottle-opener; the irony is that the imagery actually has deep roots in Balinese beliefs (penises abound in old temple carvings).

Lily Jean (p43), Seminyak

Best Clothes

Namu (p42) Nifty duds that are typical of Seminyak's fashion creativity.

Divine Diva (p42) Ultra-comfy womenswear you wished you'd packed.

Biasa (p43) One of Bali's classic fashion labels; it has an international reputation for its brilliant use of fabrics and materials.

Blue Glue (p43) Ditch that frumpy wet thing hanging over the hotel tub.

Lily Jean (p43) Sexy wisps of this and that. You'll find something fun and even daring for any time of day or night.

Goddess on the Go! (p117) Cottony cool clothes for women who want comfort and style on the road; the name sums it up.

Surfer Girl (p33) The name says it all; another of Bali's iconic surf brands.

Rip Curl (p33) Bali's epic surfer brand. Sold worldwide, why not shop at the source?

Best for Browsing

JJ Bali Button (p54) Fun for the whole family; buttons pack easy too.

Hobo (p55) Clever housewares designed and made on Bali.

Ganesha Bookshop (p116) Bali's best bookshop has carefully chosen selections.

Bathe (p42) Fun stuff for the house that smells good.

Pasar Badung (p97) Bali's large central market has it all.

Best Textiles

Anis (p97) Standout dealer of beautiful local fabrics.

Threads of Life Indonesian Textile Arts Center (p116) Handmade traditional Bali fabrics.

Best
Gay & Lesbian
Bali

Bali easily ranks as one of the most tolerant places gay and lesbian people can visit. Much of this stems from the beliefs and attitudes ingrained in the Balinese. People are accepted as they are, judging others is considered extremely rude and there's a limited macho culture where masculinity is easily threatened. Anywhere listed in this book can be considered gay-friendly.

BAY ISMOYO/AFP/GETTY IMAGES ©

The Scene

Homosexuality among visitors has a long tradition on Bali. Many of the island's most influential expatriate artists have been more-or-less openly gay.

Many Balinese openly become involved with visitors of the same sex, although this is far more common with men than with women. There is no thought given to possible social ramifications among their friends, family or neighbours. In fact Bali is something of a haven for gay people from across Indonesia.

One of the converse effects about having gay life so much a part of life on Bali is that there are relatively few 'gay' places, although many bars and clubs of Seminyak's Jl Abimanyu form a nexus of Gay Bali.

☑ **Top Tips**

▶ Homosexual behaviour is not illegal on Bali.

▶ Gay men in Indonesia are referred to as *homo,* or *gay,* and are quite distinct from the female impersonators called *waria*.

▶ In general Bali is one of the most gay-friendly destinations in Southeast Asia.

Best Gay Nightlife

Obsession (p42) Gay club with a range of music.

Bali Jo (p42) Fab drag shows draw a mixed crowd.

Best Festivals & Ceremonies

A crash of the gamelan, and traffic screeches to a halt as a mob of elegantly dressed people comes flying by bearing pyramids of fruit, tasselled parasols and a furred, masked Barong or two: it's a temple procession disappearing as suddenly as it appeared, with no more than the fleeting sparkle of gold and white silk and hibiscus petals in its wake. Dozens occur daily across Bali.

☑ Top Tip

► Ask any locals you meet what *odalan* (temple festivals) are happening. Seeing one will be a highlight of your trip, particularly if it is at a major temple. Foreigners are welcome to watch the festivities, but be unobtrusive and dress modestly.

Temple Festivals

Each of the thousands of temples on the island has a 'temple birthday' known as an **odalan**. These are celebrated once every Balinese year of 210 days or every 354 to 356 days on the *caka* calendar (yes it's bewildering, there are priests who do nothing but try to sort out the calendar).

Best Special Days

Nyepi The year's most special day is marked by total inactivity – to convince evil spirits that Bali is uninhabited, so they'll leave the island alone. The night before, huge papier-mâché monsters (*ogoh-ogoh*) go up in flames. You'll see these built by enthusiastic locals in communities island-wide in the weeks before. Held in March or early April.

Galungan One of Bali's major festivals. During a 10-day period, all the gods come down to earth for the festivities, which celebrate the death of a legendary tyrant called Mayadenawa. Barong prance from temple to temple and village to village (many of these processions consist entirely of children), and locals rejoice with feasts and visits to families.

Kuningan Culmination of Galungan, when the Balinese say thanks and goodbye to the gods. You'll see large temple ceremonies across the island – and likely be caught in long traffic queues as a result. Abandon your vehicle and join the scene. On beaches, families dressed spotlessly in white look for purification from the ocean's waters.

Best
Art

Until visitors arrived in great numbers, the acts of painting or carving were just to decorate temples and shrines as well as enrich ceremonies. Today, with galleries and craft shops everywhere, paintings are stacked up on gallery floors and you may trip over carvings from both stone and wood. Amid the tat, though, you will find beautiful work.

Painting
Balinese painting is the art form most influenced by Western ideas. Ubud's art museums and galleries have a range of beautiful paintings. Styles range from abstract works of incredible colour to beautiful and evocative representations – some highly idealised – of island life.

Crafts
Bali is a showroom of Indonesia's creativity. Carving was traditionally done for temples and the Balinese are experts, with works – such as a frog using a leaf as an umbrella – often showing their sense of humour.

Masks are a popular purchase. The mask maker must know the movements that each performer uses; the results are both dramatic and colourful.

BERNARD NAPTHINE/LONELY PLANET IMAGES ©

☑ Top Tips

▶ Bali's arts and crafts originated in honouring fertility of the land and Dewi Sri, the rice goddess.

▶ Batubulan, on the main road from south Bali to Ubud, is a major stone-carving centre. Figures line both sides of the road, and carvers can be seen in action in the many workshops.

Best Museums & Galleries

Museum Le Mayeur (p85) House and gallery of one of Bali's most influential painters.

Agung Rai Museum of Art (p106) Excellent private museum in Ubud.

Museum Puri Lukisan (p107) A great history of Balinese art.

Sukyf Arch & Art (p50) Small but exquisite gallery showing Bali's best painters.

Pasifika Museum (p79) Large museum with fine works from Bali and the region.

Neka Art Museum (p107) Has paintings by many of the local greats.

Museum Bali (p95) Island's main museum has art from the ages.

Survival Guide

Survival Guide

Before You Go

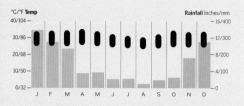

When to Go

°C/°F Temp
40/104 —
30/86 —
20/68 —
10/50 —
0/32 —

J F M A M J J A S O N D

Rainfall Inches/mm
— 16/400
— 12/300
— 8/200
— 4/100
— 0

➡ **High Season (Jul & Aug)** Rates zip up by 50% or more; many hotels are booked far ahead. Christmas and New Year are equally expensive and crowded.

➡ **Shoulder (May, Jun & Sep)** Coincides with the best weather (drier, less humid); some deals but last-minute bookings possible; best time for diving, since the water is clear.

➡ **Low Season (Jan-Apr, Oct & Nov)** Deals everywhere; rainy season, however, rainfall is rarely excessive.

Book Your Stay

➡ It's common for people to move around Bali, even for short stays. Splitting your time between, say, Seminyak and Ubud is typical.

➡ Ubud is best enjoyed staying overnight, after daytrippers are gone and dance performances are on.

➡ With a budget of $100 a night you can find nice midrange hotels virtually everywhere (often for much less).

➡ Villas (see p51) can be surprisingly affordable: for under US$200 you can have your own small compound.

Useful Websites
See p51 for additional websites for villa bookings.

Bali Discovery (www.balidiscovery.com) Has discount rates for hundreds of places.

Asia Rooms (www.asiarooms.com) Good for rooms in the region.

Agoda (www.agoda.com) Often good for last-minute details.

Lonely Planet (www.lonelyplanet.com) Author recommendations, reviews and online bookings.

Best Budget

Mimpi Bungalows (kumimpi@yahoo.com.sg; Kuta) Lush gardens boast orchids and shade, and the pool is a good size.

Inada Losmen (putuinada@hotmail.com; Seminyak) This budget champ is a short walk from clubs, the beach and other Seminyak joys.

Nirvana Pension & Gallery (www.nirvanaku.com; Ubud) There are *alang alang* (woven thatch) roofs, a plethora of paintings and ornate doorways, in a shady, secluded locale.

Best Midrange

Tony's Villa (www.balitonys.com; Seminyak) Beaches and some of Bali's best restaurants are just minutes from Tony's. Fairly modest bungalow-style units are part of a compound with slightly more lavish villas.

Mu (www.mu-bali.com; Bingin) Stylish and very individual bungalows with round, pointed thatched roofs are scattered about a compound dominated by a cliffside infinity pool.

Mutiara Bali (www.mutiarabali.com; Seminyak) Close to fine dining (two minutes) and the beach (five minutes). Rooms surround a frangipani-draped pool area.

Oka Wati Hotel (www.okawatihotel.com; Ubud) Oka Wati (the owner) is a lovely lady who grew up near the Ubud Palace. Rooms have large verandas where the delightful staff will deliver your choice of breakfast.

Matahari Cottages (www.matahariubud.com; Ubud) Flamboyant, themed rooms include the 'Batavia Princess' and the 'Indian Pasha'. High tea is elaborately served on silver.

Alam Indah (www.alamindahbali.com; Ubud) This isolated and spacious resort has rooms that are beautifully finished in natural materials to traditional designs; great views.

Best Top End

Oberoi (www.oberoihotels.com; Seminyak) Beautifully understated, all accommodations have private verandahs; also private villas, ocean views and private walled pools. Fine beachfront.

Warwick Ibah Luxury Villas (www.warwickibah.com; Ubud) Overlooking the rushing waters of the Wos Valley, stylish individual suites and villas are filled with art and antiques.

Amandari (www.amanresorts.com; Ubud) Does everything with charm and grace – sort of like a classical Balinese dancer. Superb views over the jungle and down to the river.

Arriving in Bali

☑ **Top Tip** For the best way to get to your accommodation from Bali's airport, see p17. Also see the Getting There & Around section at the start of each regional chapter for taxi prices.

Ngurah Rai Airport

➡ Prepaid taxis from Bali's airport are the most common way to get to your accommodation.

➡ Most hotels will pick you up at the airport for a fee from US$5 to US$50 (typical for the fairly long haul to Ubud). This can be especially nice if you are arriving after a long flight and/or it's your first visit to Bali. A hotel rep will be waiting in the arrivals area with your name written on a sign-board.

➡ Unless you absolutely, positively need help with your bags, refuse the service of the arrivals area porters as fees can be surprising (if needed, negotiate a price in advance).

➡ And when you're departing, have 150,000Rp in exact change for your departure tax.

Getting Around

Taxi

☑ **Best for**... Most trips.

➡ Bali taxis are plentiful and surprisingly cheap.

They are the preferred means of travel for most trips around south Bali.

➡ Always insist on the meter and get out of any cab that refuses.

➡ The most reliable company remains **Bluebird Taxi** (📞0361-701111); you can call for pickup. Look for the 'Bluebird Group' sticker over the windshield (many other taxis try to ape the look).

Car & Driver

☑ **Best for**... Maximum flexibility, minimal fuss.

➡ For a fee of US$40 to US$60 per day you can arrange for a driver with a vehicle to take you virtually anywhere you want to go on Bali. This lets you go where you want when you want to and you can stop off wherever you want. It's easiest to arrange this through your accommodation.

➡ Most drivers are charming people who will add delight to your journey; however, if your driver pressures you to stop for food at a tourist restaurant surrounded by tour buses or any kind of souvenir shop, refuse. They are probably getting a kickback; use a different driver next time.

Car

☑ **Best for**... Exploring completely on your own.

➡ Car rentals cost US$25 to US$50 per day. Offers are everywhere. However, you'll have to deal with Bali's horrendous traffic and myriad ways to get lost.

Motorbike

☑ **Best for**... Saving money, beating traffic.

➡ Offers to rent motorbikes are everywhere. Daily costs are US$5 to US$20. If you are a skilled rider, you can weave around traffic, but helmets are required and accidents are very common. Some motorbikes come equipped with surfboard racks.

Tourist Bus

☑ **Best for**... Saving money.

➡ **Perama** (www.peramatour .com) runs air-con buses (about 100,000Rp) for tourists between Kuta, Sanur, Ubud and points east. But the buses don't come close to Seminyak, Kerobokan etc or anyplace on the Bukit Peninsula such as Ulu Watu or Nusa Dua. And the stops are sometimes inconvenient.

Essential Information

....

Business Hours

It is assumed that standard hours are as follows. Significant variations are shown in the listings.

Restaurants and cafes
8am to 10pm daily

Shops and services catering to visitors 9am to 8pm daily

Electricity

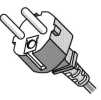

220V/230V/50Hz

220V/230V/50Hz

Emergency

If you have a problem that needs police or medical attention, ask at the nearest hotel or restaurant as there are no useful central numbers for visitors to call.

Health

☑ **Top Tip** Do not drink tap water; opt for cheaply available bottled water (and refill and reuse bottles when possible). Ice in tourist places is normally made with filtered water at a central plant – if it is uniform in shape, it should be safe.

➡ There are several clinics and hospitals in south Bali that have Western standards. The most popular – and expensive – is **BIMC** (☎0361-761263; www.bimcbali.com; Jl Ngurah Rai 100X). Hotels can make recommendations.

➡ Ensure that you have travel insurance that covers medical evacuation.

➡ Rabies is a major problem on Bali; if you are bitten or come into contact with a stray animal, seek medical attention immediately as rabies is fatal.

➡ Dengue fever is a problem; wear mosquito repellents that contains DEET.

➡ Travellers diarrhoea is common. Stay hydrated and, if it doesn't improve in 24 hours, consider antibiotics from a pharmacy.

Money

☑ **Top Tip** You can use ATMs as your source for money for your entire trip. Bring US$100 in case the network goes down or there is a problem with your card and you need backup.

➡ Indonesia's unit of currency is the rupiah (Rp). There are coins worth 50Rp, 100Rp, 500Rp and 1000Rp. Notes come in denominations of 1000Rp, 5000Rp, 10,000Rp, 20,000Rp, 50,000Rp and 100,000Rp.

➡ US dollars are the most convertible currency.

➡ Always carry a good supply of rupiah in small denominations. Individuals will struggle to make change for a 50,000Rp note or larger.

ATMs
➡ There are ATMs all over Bali (with the notable exception of Nusa Lembongan); Circle K convenience stores are reliable locations.

➡ Exchange rates for ATM withdrawals are usually okay, but see if your home bank will hit you with outrageous fees.

Credit Cards
➡ Visa, MasterCard and Amex are accepted by most larger businesses.

Moneychangers
➡ Exchange rates offered by moneychangers with signs along the road may seem better than banks, but that's because the difference is often made up through scams.

➡ Change money at banks, although this

can be time-consuming. Avoid this hassle and use an ATM.

Tipping
➡ Tipping a set percentage is not expected in Bali, but if the service is good, it's appropriate to leave 5000Rp or 10% or more.

➡ Most midrange hotels and restaurants and all top-end hotels and restaurants add 21% to the bill for tax and service (known as 'plus plus'). This service component is distributed among hotel staff (one hopes).

➡ Hand cash directly to individuals if you think they deserve recognition for their service.

➡ Tip good taxi drivers, guides, people giving you a massage or fetching you a beer on the beach etc; 5000Rp to 10,000Rp is generous.

Public Holidays
☑ **Top Tip** Check if Nyepi falls during your trip as Bali shuts down entirely for 24 hours.

The following holidays are celebrated throughout Indonesia. Many of the dates change according to the phase of the moon

(not by month) or by religious calendar, so the following are estimates only.

➡ **Tahun Baru Masehi** (New Year's Day) 1 January

➡ **Idul Adha** (Muslim festival of sacrifice) February

➡ **Muharram** (Islamic New Year) February/March

➡ **Nyepi** (Hindu New Year) March/April

➡ **Hari Paskah** (Good Friday) April

➡ **Ascension of Christ** April/May

➡ **Hari Waisak** (Buddha's birth, enlightenment and death) April/May

➡ **Maulud Nabi Mohammed/Hari Natal** (Prophet Mohammed's birthday) May

➡ **Hari Proklamasi Kemerdekaan** (Indonesian Independence Day) 17 August

➡ **Isra Miraj Nabi Mohammed** (Ascension of the Prophet Mohammed) September

➡ **Idul Fitri** (End of Ramadan) November/December

➡ **Hari Natal** (Christmas Day) 25 December

Safe Travel

☑ **Top Tip** Bali is fairly safe, so relax and enjoy your trip.

➡ Violent crime is uncommon, but bag-snatching, pickpocketing and theft from rooms and parked cars is increasing. Take sensible precautions as you would in a major city.

➡ Don't take drugs to Bali nor buy any while there. Penalties are severe.

➡ Avoid beaches and the ocean around streams running into the water after rain – all sorts of unsavoury matter may be present.

➡ Be careful when walking on the sidewalk or pavement; sudden gaping holes can cause severe injury. Carry a torch/flashlight at night.

Telephone

☑ **Top Tip** If a Bali phone number doesn't work, try adding a 4 between the area code (eg 0361) and the number. Extra digits are being added to numbers to allow for more lines through 2014. Automated prompts announcing a number change don't always work. See p45 for more.

➡ SIM cards for your unlocked GSM mobile phone on Bali cost only 50,000Rp. They come with cheap rates for calling other countries, starting at US$0.20 per minute. You can buy them everywhere, just ask.

➡ If you don't have a local SIM card for your mobile, roaming rates can be outrageous.

➡ Most hotel wi-fi service in south Bali and Ubud will allow Skype to work.

Phone Codes

Directory assistance	☎108
Indonesia country code	☎62
International call prefix	☎001/017
International operator	☎102

Toilets

➡ Western-style toilets are almost universally common in tourist areas.

➡ During the day, look for a cafe or hotel and smile (public toilets only exist at some major sights).

Visas

☑ **Top Tip** Carry US$25 in exact change for the visa on arrival at Bali's airport.

➡ Citizens of over 60 countries, including all major ones, can purchase a visa on arrival at Bali's airport for US$25. It is good for 30 days. To confirm if your country is included, check this website: www.embassy ofindonesia.org/ consular/voa.htm.

Index

See also separate subindexes for:

🗙 **Eating p157**

🍷 **Drinking p158**

✪ **Entertainment p158**

🛍 **Shopping p158**

☒ Eating

Behind the Scenes

Send Us Your Feedback

We love to hear from travellers – your comments help make our books better. We read every word, and we guarantee that your feedback goes straight to the authors. Visit **lonelyplanet.com/contact** to submit your updates and suggestions.

Note: We may edit, reproduce and incorporate your comments in Lonely Planet products such as guidebooks, websites and digital products, so let us know if you don't want your comments reproduced or your name acknowledged. For a copy of our privacy policy visit lonelyplanet.com/privacy.

Our Readers

Many thanks to the travellers who used the last edition and wrote to us with helpful hints, useful advice and interesting anecdotes:

Christian Cantos, Dirk Dillinger, Claire Wilkinson, Edwin Woltering

Ryan's Thanks

Many thanks to wonderful Bali friends like Hanafi, Eliot Cohen, Jamie James, Ibu Cat, Patricia 'Patticakes' Miklautsch, Pascal and Pika, Nengah and Made, Marilyn, Stuart McDonald and everyone else who made beautiful music for me. In Portland a special shout-out to Annah, who shall always be in my heart.

Acknowledgments

Cover photograph: Bali's sacred mountain, Gunung Agung, viewed from Sanur Beach at sunrise, and traditional outrigger canoe, Sheldon Lewis/Getty Images. Many of the images in this guide are available for licensing from Lonely Planet Images: www.lonelyplanetimages.com.

This Book

This 3rd edition of Lonely Planet's *Pocket Bali* guidebook was researched and written by Ryan Ver Berkmoes. This guidebook was commissioned in Lonely Planet's Melbourne office, and produced by the following:

Commissioning Editors Ilaria Walker, Rebecca Currie **Coordinating Editor** Andrea Dobbin **Coordinating Cartographer** Rachel Imeson **Coordinating Layout Designer** Carol Jackson **Managing Editor** Annelies Mertens **Senior Editors** Susan Paterson, Andi Jones **Managing Cartographers** Shahara Ahmed, Corey Hutchison

Managing Layout Designer Chris Girdler **Cover Research** Naomi Parker **Internal Image Research** Claire Gibson, Rebecca Skinner **Thanks to** Imogen Bannister, Sasha Baskett, Nicholas Colicchia, Bruce Evans, Ryan Evans, Anna Lorincz, Trent Paton, Kirsten Rawlings, Averil Robertson, Laura Stansfeld, Gerard Walker

Our Writer

Ryan Ver Berkmoes

Ryan Ver Berkmoes was first entranced by the echoing beat of a Balinese gamelan in 1993. On his visits since he has explored almost every corner of the island, watching places like Bingin Beach change from unknown strips of sand to favoured spots of visitor joy. And just when he thinks Bali holds no more surprises, he finds, for example, a small road leading down to a beach and fishing village on nobody's map. Away from Bali, Ryan has written about destinations worldwide and covered everything from wars to bars; he definitely prefers the latter. Read more at www.ryanverberkmoes.com.

Published by Lonely Planet Publications Pty Ltd
ABN 36 005 607 983
3rd edition – Nov 2012
ISBN 978 1 74220 211 2
© Lonely Planet 2012   Photographs © as indicated 2012
10 9 8 7 6 5 4 3 2 1
Printed in China